ROY A. MEDVEDEV: POLITICAL ESSAYS

Roy A. Medvedev
Political Essays

EUROPEAN SOCIALIST THOUGHT SERIES No. 8

SPOKESMAN BOOKS

Published by the Bertrand Russell Peace Foundation Ltd., Bertrand Russell House, Gamble Street, Nottingham for
Spokesman Books
Printed by the Russell Press, Nottingham

Acknowledgements

The bulk of the essays in this volume were translated by Tamara
Deutscher, who is responsible for the English versions of chapters
1, 3, 4, 6, 7, 9 and 10. Brian Pearce translated chapter 5, and Marilyn
Vogt chapter 2. Chapter 11 was translated by Reuben Ainsztein.
Chapters 1, 5 and 8 were first published in *New Left Review*. Chapter
2 appeared first in *Intercontinental Press*. Part of chapter 11 was
published in *The Sunday Times*.

The Bertrand Russell Peace Foundation is grateful to the editors
of all these publications for their kind permission to permit reproduc-
tion of those sections of this book which have previously been
published in their pages. Thanks are also due to all the translators,
and to Zhores Medvedev for his unfailingly kind assistance.

Contents

Series Introduction

Having passed through a veritable Dark Age, in which dogmatism and obscurantism held a world-wide predominance, and flourished alongside small-minded provinciality, socialist thought has, during the past two decades, undergone a veritable renaissance, affecting almost every major European country, East or West. The collapse of Stalinist orthodoxy has been accompanied by a renewal of radical thinking in some of the older social-democratic and communist parties, and the growth of several independent schools of young intellectuals who have been profoundly influenced by ideals of socialist humanism.

Unfortunately, much of the most audacious and relevant thinking in France, Italy, Hungary, Yugoslavia, Belgium and Germany has been kept out of reach in Britain by a combination of difficulties: commercial publishers have been conservative in taking on commitments unless the authors in question have been glamorous, publicity-attractive figures; all those works which have had a strong empirical base in the experience of a national labour movement have tended to escape translation because it is widely assumed that the English-speaking public is not interested in the detailed sociology of other European countries; and the specialist socialist publishing houses have been highly selective in their choice of doctrinal filters for a variety of reasons.

Extracts from the writings of such men as Mallet, Marković or Goldmann have been featured in the periodical press in Britain, and some of the specialist works of these authors have found respectable imprints. But not only have major works escaped translation: so too have numerous practical, polemical and agitational writings, some of which are very great interest to all socialists.

The object of this series is to begin to remedy some of these deficiencies. It is hoped to make available a number of important original works of analysis as well as some more directly propagandist essays which will assist the Labour Movements of the English-speaking world to understand their colleagues. But it is also hoped that the series may assist in widening the dialogue between socialists in East and West Europe, and emphasising the organic unity of their interests and concerns.

Ken Coates

Other Titles In The
European Socialist Thought Series:

Part1

Problems of Détente and Socialist Democracy

1: Democracy and Détente

Some four to five years ago the international situation was still a source of serious anxiety to all who cared for peace, democracy and socialism. The enormous scale of the continuous American intervention in Indochina, the incursion of the Warsaw Pact troops into the territory of the Czechoslovak Socialist Republic, the new Berlin crisis, the armed skirmishes on the Soviet-Chinese border, the acceleration of the arms race all over the world — all these were exacerbating international tensions to the utmost, and encouraging reactionary and extremist forces in every country. Major efforts were needed to change the trend of world events. Today, we know that such efforts were made and that they have achieved quite impressive results. We shall not enumerate here all the agreements and treaties which have critically altered the international atmosphere. It should not be overlooked, however, that the progress of détente over the last three years has been neither smooth nor easy. Initiatives of the USSR have played a very significant role in furthering it. We can assume that the development of the Soviet 'peace offensive' provoked serious disagreements among our leaders.

The main reason for the elimination of Shelest, for example, was certainly not because of his 'nationalist' errors, but because of his objections to Nixon's trip to the USSR in 1972. The pensioning-off of Voronov from the Politbureau was another major setback to rightist circles within our leadership.

International détente was not, of course, the outcome of the Soviet peace offensive alone. It was made possible by mutual concessions, and readiness to compromise on both sides. It is plain that in the Western countries this readiness for compromise likewise emerged only after prolonged and acute political conflicts. The diminution of international tension created conditions not only for limiting *increases* in strategic armaments, but also for *reducing* the military establishments of all the great powers and of many smaller countries, and thereby for accelerating the peaceful economic development of every continent. The improvement of relations between the largest powers on the planet has thus proceeded not at the expense of other countries and nations; it benefits all mankind.

The Current Repression

In the past, the state of armed confrontation between the Great Powers, the 'Cold War' and the debased anti-Soviet and anti-Western propaganda which they exchanged in no way helped to overcome the remnants of Stalinist totalitarianism nor to foster democratic reforms in the USSR. Today, however, we can likewise see that international détente and development of trade and other forms of co-operation, do not automatically lead to changes in the political climate in the Soviet Union, to the growth of democratic freedoms, or to respect for the political and civic rights of the individual, either.

No country in the world has in this century undergone such dramatic and contradictory experiences as the Soviet Union. It was therefore natural that even the insignificant and limited degree of democratization which could be observed in our country between 1961 and 1967, awoke among thinking elements in our society the most diverse political currents, both within the framework of Marxism and without it. Although these trends involved only a minimal fraction of our intelligentsia, this awakening of political thought alarmed the Right within the leadership of the CPSU. This wing of the party is composed of functionaries promoted and formed in the epoch when Soviet society was plunged in utter political passivity and silence, when administrative rather than political methods, coercion rather than persuasion, were used to rule the country.

Various measures to constrict freedom of political discussion within the USSR were introduced by 1967 and at the beginning of 1968. They were notably tightened after August 1968. All political tendencies, 'left' as well as 'right', were attacked, although in differing degree; in recent years, for instance, the most blatant manifestations of Russian chauvinism and open exaltations of Stalin have also been condemned. Subsequent foreign policy successes of the Soviet Union and the slackening of international tension did not put a stop to the assault on 'dissenters'.

In many respects, the pressure against dissent even increased; political trends that had only just started to emerge were stifled and social thought repressed. A considerable number of people, who had much to say, were forced into silence as they were not prepared to put at risk their own apparent freedom or the well-being of their relatives and friends.

This pressure from above in no way excluded recourse to straightforward judicial repressions or even to such inhuman methods of intimidation as shutting sane people up in psychiatric hospitals for patently political reasons. The words and deeds of broken men like Yakir and Krasin were exploited to disintegrate and demoralize oppositionists of past years. Many Western papers long presented Yakir and Krasin as 'courageous fighters for human rights', although the unprincipled and objectively provocative character of their activity had been obvious to a number of people in our country for some years. The strength of various democratic tendencies was also reduced by the noticeable easing of emigration to Israel. Under the influence of the new situation, even those Jews and their relatives who not long before had actively worked for the enlargement of civil rights and liberties in the USSR and had no intention of leaving the country, began to emigrate. Very recently, dispatch abroad of dissenters from other non-Jewish nationalities has also begun, although still experimentally.

For the majority of ordinary 'unorthodox' people or those inclined to be critical of certain aspects of our political and social life, the mounting administrative pressure against all dissent is, however, of the greatest importance. As is well known, in our country the State is not merely the main, it is in fact the only 'employer'. In the absence of all democratic checks or balances, this circumstance affords extremely simple and highly effective means of exerting pressure on people who perform their professional work irreproachably, but are not 'loyal' enough in the opinion of one or another high official. Protests against the restriction of democratic rights in the USSR continues to this day, of course. In some respects they have even intensified and assumed new forms. These protests are, however, more and more made by individuals or, at best, by very small groups of people who are protected not so much by democratic traditions or institutions, as by their international reputation and fame. Such people now come forward in a much more active and resolute manner than was possible even for them some years before: they publish their artistic or scientific writings abroad, are interviewed by foreign correspondents, release public statements widely disseminated beyond our frontiers. The activity of these people now arouses a much greater political resonance than ever before, and has become an important element in our political life. Their courage cannot be doubted, and it deserves respect.

Recent Statements by Leading Dissenters

However, it is necessary also to be aware that many of these people live under constant and intense pressure, that they are subjected to crude and unjust abuse in the press and in propaganda by word of mouth, that they are painfully hurt by the persecution and arrests of their less famous colleagues and friends. Deprived of the previous support that has sustained them in a somewhat wider circle of intelligentsia, many of them have begun to express more and more extremist viewpoints, to put forward less and less constructive proposals, being moved more by emotions than by the considerations of political efficacy.

One man, for instance, recently claimed that even blacks in South Africa are not subjected to such cruel persecution and constriction as 'unorthodox thinkers' in the USSR. Another attacked Brandt bitterly and unjustly for his *Ostpolitik,* declaring that Brandt was betraying the interests of democracy in the West and in the East, and that he should be tried by a future Nuremberg Tribunal for war crimes. A third told his friends that Allende's government had led Chile into an impasse from which the only way out was either a 'red' or a 'white' dictatorship, and that in such a situation the military putsch, even with its excesses, was 'the lesser evil' for Chile and its people. A fourth appealed to the American Congress not to encourage trade with the USSR until the Soviet Union conceded full freedom of emigration, as if this were the minimum demand of democracy. Yet it is perfectly obvious that, although the right to leave a country is an important civic freedom, it is much more important to create conditions in the Soviet Union such that its citizens should not desire to leave their own country.

Opinions and statements of this kind, widely publicized in the Western press, are now undoubtedly arousing not only reserve but reprobation among left-wing and democratic circles in the West. At the same time they are also being exploited by reactionary groups in the leadership of our country to increase the pressure on the intelligentsia, and to split and demoralize the ranks of the 'dissenters'.

The clamp-down on the intelligentsia became pronounced at the end of August and the beginning of September 1973, when the Soviet press launched a violent campaign against one of our greatest scientists, the atomic physicist Academician Andrei Sakharov. This assault was also partly directed against the oustanding Russian writer Alexander Solzhenitsyn. What was the background of this campaign? Sakharov and Solzhenitsyn, independently of each other, had given interviews to foreign correspondents in which they expressed their views on many topical questions of international politics and on some concrete internal problems of the Soviet Union. The opinions which the two men expressed were by no means incontrovertible. In itself, therefore, the mere fact that Soviet newspapers published letters from individual readers, or even certain collective communications, criticizing one or other of Sakharov's or Solzhenitsyn's contentions, was not extraordinary. What was objectionable, however, was the fact that in these 'indignant protests' the statements and opinions of Sakharov were largely distorted, while the substance of Solzhenitsyn's declaration was simply suppressed altogether. The overwhelming majority of academicians, writers, workers, employees or technicians who signed these protests, were not acquainted with the full text of the interviews given by either Sakharov or Solzhenitsyn; at best they were shown only some sentences from them taken out of context. We know that many people who did sign the collective declarations were subjected to intense pressures, and that the majority of them had not the slightest idea why Sakharov and Solzhenitsyn gave these interviews to Western correspondents. The main aim of those who organized this vociferous campaign was not to silence Sakharov and Solzhenitsyn; their primary objective was to maximize pressure on other less known 'dissidents' and on the bulk of the thinking intelligentsia. To some extent the campaign obviously achieved this aim, but it had far less success than its initiators had expected.

Explanations of the Clamp-Down

Of course, the aggravation of various forms of harassment of 'dissidents' in the last few months, was not a direct result of the gradual international détente. Yet it does seem that there was a connection between the two processes. It has been suggested, for example, that all the clumsy ideological campaigns of recent months were unleashed by right-wing dogmatic tendencies within the Central Committee of the CPSU independently of the main leadership in the Politbureau, and that the real purpose of these campaigns was to halt the Soviet 'peace offensive' in the international arena, and in particular to disrupt the European Security Conference. This hypothesis rests on the belief that our own 'hawks' sought to provoke a combination of domestic developments and foreign protests against them, of a sort that would inevitably put a stop to any prospect of rapprochement and break up international détente. The result would be to arrest incipient scientific and technical co-operation between the USSR and the West, and to revive the acrimonious polemics with the West, which give the extreme Right of our leadership a particular feeling of well-being.

However, there is another interpretation of the campaign that is more plausible. Wide-ranging economic co-operation with capitalist countries, abolition of traditional barriers to trade and tourism, limitation and reduction of weapons and armed forces, winding down of the 'Cold War', and in consequence improvement of East-West contacts, naturally demand more mutual confidence at least in international relations. This in turn cannot but affect the field of ideology. A real end to the 'Cold War' and an improvement in the international climate is quite impossible – indeed unthinkable – without the liquidation of all discrimination not only in trade, but also in exchange of information and contact between peoples. The development of international collaboration cannot be achieved without broadening the exchange of men and information; and what is needed to achieve this is, in the first instance, a number of definite concessions on our part – for example, the elimination of such archaic remnants of the Cold War as jamming of foreign radio stations. As is known, the Soviet State broadcasts in all the main languages of the globe, giving its point of view on all world events and also presenting and interpreting developments in our own country. In these circumstances, jamming of Western radio stations which in their transmissions have a different ideological standpoint but a similar functional aim, is discrimination which hinders the process of détente just as much as the possible refusal of the US Congress to grant us the status of 'most favoured nation' in trade.

This concession has already been made: from 21 September 1973 the jamming of the Voice of America, of the BBC, and of the *Deutsche Welle* has ceased. Apparently more facilities will be granted to foreign correspondents in the USSR: they will be able to travel about the country and to make contacts with Soviet citizens. Journalists will have the same rights and facilities as all Soviet correspondents abroad have long had at their disposal. Next on the agenda for settlement will be the question of the reception of American television programmes on Soviet sets and vice versa, transmitted live by satellite; as also that of granting the Soviet people greater opportunities to read Western newspapers, journals, scientific literature, etc. The ratification – long overdue – of UN Charters of social, cultural, economic, political and civic rights is also a positive development.

Obviously, international exchange of ideas and persons calls for a modification of forms and methods of ideological work in the Soviet Union, a greater flexibility in our propaganda and a moratorium on antiquated and dogmatic pronouncements: in other words it calls for a development of Marxism. Under present conditions of ideological struggle, Marxism can only retain influence on the consciousness of people – let alone increase it – by uncompromisingly honest, open and truthful scientific analysis of the totality of contemporary social problems and of the whole unfalsified history of international events and revolutionary experiences of the 20th century.

It is a noticeable fact that the officials and organizations in our country which are in charge of economic questions, foreign affairs and external trade, have proved to be better equipped to work in new conditions than those assigned to ideological problems. Many of the latter have proved incapable of extending the Soviet 'peace offensive' into the ideological arena for which they are responsible. Clearly driven on to the defensive, with no prospects of influencing popular consciousness, our leading ideologues try to cope with new tasks not by adopting new decisions, but by strengthening 'ideological discipline', by intimidating dissenters, by increasing political and moral pressure on Soviet citizens – in other words, not by persuasion but by duress, which in the end is fatal to any ideology.

Factional Struggles within the Party

The contradiction inherent in this situation, and the discrepancies in the handling of external and internal problems (discrepancies which were virtually non-existent in August 1968, but which are very evident today), provide the soil for polemical disputes and factional struggles within the higher echelons of the Central Committee of the CPSU. This type of conflict tends to generate internal mutual accommodation: it is possible that the heightening of pressure on 'dissenters' and the recent laborious campaigns against unorthodoxy were precisely concessions made to the right wing of our leadership in exchange for acceptance of a foreign policy of détente and trade with the West. All this is no more than a hypothesis, of course. The possibility cannot be discounted that no such compromise has occurred, but rather that the entire Politbureau is convinced that only intensification of struggle on the 'ideological front' can fortify this 'front' at home against the prospect of a détente inevitably linked to increased international exchange of men and ideas.

The activity of rightist, reactionary and dogmatic forces in the USSR has not been confined to the 'affair' of Sakharov and Solzhenitsyn; it also left its mark on all the discussions of problems within the social sciences in the first half of 1973. We have been witnessing an obvious deterioration in the field of historical writing, in philosophy, in the debates on many economic problems, as well as in literature and art. This outburst of activity on the Right was undoubtedly occasioned by the détente, which not only seemed dangerous to reactionary forces but actually is dangerous to them, because it weakens their influence in all countries which pass from the phase of confrontation to that of co-operation. In the Soviet Union, however, where moderate and more sober politicians sit in the same Central Committee together with blatant reactionaries and where the struggle is conducted, unseen by society, behind closed doors in the 'corridors of power' — in such conditions the conflict between various groups and tendencies is accompanied by an unmistakeable 'cooling' of the whole internal political atmosphere.

How can these regressive tendencies in our internal politics be overcome? In what way can the growing weight of reactionary forces of the Right on cultural and ideological life in the USSR be weakened? The answer to these questions is not easy. There are certainly no quick solutions to the problem. It is clear that the forces of the progressive intelligentsia, including the Party intelligentsia, are still too feeble to oppose the sharp swing to the right in our political and social life. It is also necessary to take into account the political passivity of the working class, of the employees, and even more so of the peasantry. In the apparatus of the Party and the State there are not a few sober people who realize the necessity of changes in domestic politics, but these 'party-democratic' groups have little influence and usually occupy the lower rungs of the official hierarchy.

Change from Above and Change from Below

Any shift towards a more consistent democratization, towards greater tolerance to the 'dissenters', towards a more flexible and reasonable internal policy that would permit the existence of political minorities both inside and outside the framework of Marxism, is at present possible in the USSR only as a result of certain initiatives 'from above' supported 'from below', but not as a sheer result of pressure from 'below'. The need for a thorough-going democratization of Soviet society has long since arrived in the USSR. It is, in fact, the most important precondition for an acceleration of the economic, political, social and cultural development of our country. Only a genuine socialist democracy can give birth to the new motor forces that are necessary to restore health and life to the whole system of Soviet institutions and organizations. The political passivity of our population 'below' is, however, equally obvious. People have learnt to become so silent, and have acquired such a sense of guilt, that no individual dissenters — not even small groups of dissenters — can give rise to a mass movement capable of bringing about any real political change. The masses could move only as a result of serious political or economic crises. Yet the prospect of such crises seems neither probable nor desirable. Soviet society can and will develop even within its existing political structure and economic conditions. Although its development is too slow by the yardstick of the real possibilities of socialism, it is nevertheless sufficient to avert any incontrollable growth of dissatisfaction among broad masses of the people. The economic resources and the natural wealth of the Soviet Union are so great, and the State monopoly of foreign trade safeguards our domestic market so well from undesirable competition, that even under a weak and incompetent leadership, growth in all branches of the national economy will continue.

In such conditions a reorganization of social and economic management, an enlargement of political and civic liberties, an expansion of socialist democracy, can come — as we have said — not as a result of open pressure by the popular masses and the intelligentsia, but as a consequence of initiatives 'from above'. In effect, the exposure of the 'cult of personality' of Stalin at the 20th Congress of the CPSU was in no sense the result of a simple pressure of the masses or the lower ranks of the party. This event, so important for the fate of the whole world communist movement, was the result of some certain struggles 'at the top' whose details have still to be fully clarified, and which reflected a growing dissatisfaction in the country only very obliquely. Likewise, the undeniable 'liberalization', the noticeable loosening of censorship in all fields of intellectual and artistic creativity, as well as many other positive processes which unfolded for some years after the 22nd Congress, were in the first instance the work of the political 'height'. Of course, the majority of our intelligentsia welcomed the 'thaw', which warmed the atmosphere of our country. However, only a small section of the intelligentsia hastened to avail itself of this 'liberalization', which was why in the sphere of creation of new spiritual values, the results were noticeable, but not very considerable. The majority adopted a waiting attitude, fearing — as it turned out, not without reason — that the 'thaw' might prove temporary and would soon be succeeded by a new period of 'inclemency' in our cultural life.

But if today it is not the outlook of those 'below' that is of decisive importance, but the moods and views of those 'above', how can the political 'heights' be impelled to proceed not towards a further 'tightening of the screws', but towards an enlargement of socialist democracy? It is true, of course, that there exists among the broad masses as well as among the intelligentsia of the USSR a growing frustration and dissatisfaction with many aspects of our society: with the slow tempo of our economic, social, and cultural progress, with our overcentralized and bureaucratized system of management, with waste of resources and lack of information, with failure to catch up with the West in so many respects, and so on. This mass discontent has an effect in very complicated and roundabout ways on the leadership of the country too. However, the higher one goes in the ruling hierarchy, the less this pressure of popular dissatisfaction is felt; which is why it cannot lead to swift changes towards democracy.

The Ambiguity of External Pressures

Thus the idea of increasing pressure from outside tends involuntarily to occur. The impact and influence which international opinion has on the ruling circles of one 'or another big or small country should not be underestimated. The general indignation provoked in the West by the introduction of the 'tax on learning' imposed on emigrants (at present, of course, the majority of emigrants are Jews), the numerous protests of public figures and organizations, the debate on the subject in the US Congress, etc. — all these reactions led the Soviet leadership to drop this tax, although formally it has not been annulled. Likewise, it was not the remonstrations of Soviet scientists but the determined protests of Western scientists and academic institutions against the onset of a shrill campaign to discredit Academician Sakharov and prepare the ground for his expulsion from the Academy of Sciences of the USSR (the demand for which had already appeared in many articles), that has saved this outstanding Soviet scientist, at least for the time being, from repression. Again, it was not public opinion in the USSR, still less our community of writers, but the enormous international prestige of Solzhenitsyn as a Nobel Prize winner that has restrained the right-wing of the Soviet leadership from settling its accounts with this eminent Russian writer.

At the same time, it is only fair to remark that it was precisely the prolonged pressure not only of American, but also of international public opinion, that eventually helped to bring direct American military intervention in Indochina to an end. Equally, we should not overlook the connection between the recent amnesty granted to political prisoners in Greece and the long struggle of the progressive forces in Europe for the re-establishment of a democratic regime in Greece. Other examples of the genuine influence of international public opinion on the course of political events in one country or another could be adduced; although there is also still a very long list of sombre and tragic occurrences which the public opinion of the West, of the East or even of the whole world, has unfortunately proved only too helpless to avert.

But in one way or another, public opinion constitutes an important force with which any politician today must reckon, including the Soviet leaders. However, it would be a great oversimplification to suppose that it is only with the assistance of pressure from outside, let alone in the field of international relations and trade, that genuine concessions can be gained in the internal politics of a country like the Soviet Union. Pressure from outside can play both a positive and a negative role. It may in some cases restrain our agencies of power from certain deeds, and in other cases it may, on the contrary, provoke them into undesirable action and thereby hinder the democratization of Soviet society.

Thus, for example, it would be unreal to suppose that under pressure from the US Congress the Soviet government would pass a special law allowing everybody who desires to do so to emigrate from the USSR. If the American Congress were to adopt the Jackson Amendment and withdraw the 'most favoured nation' clause in trade relations, this would not improve but harm the prospects of further emigration. Soviet-American relations would also deteriorate. At present work on the draft of a new Constitution for the USSR is in progress. Significant improvements in the sections concerning the civic and political rights of Soviet citizens, and the constitutional guarantees of these rights, are envisaged. The authors of the draft cannot now avoid dealing with such an important democratic freedom as the right to leave one's country and return to it at will. However formal many constitutional rights of Soviet citizens may be, the inclusion in the new Constitution, even with certain reservations, of rights of free entry and exit in the USSR would be extremely important. The adoption by the US Congress of the Jackson Amendment would only lessen the chances of such a clause being included in the new Constitution. For this reason, we consider Academician Sakharov's appeal to American Congressmen to support this amendment to be a mistaken step, both tactically and substantively.

Appeals to the Western Right

In general, it would be wrong to overestimate the possibility of achieving results by exercising pressure on the USSR in the field of diplomatic or economic relations, and not merely because the Soviet side would reasonably object to interference in the internal affairs of the USSR. We very much doubt that the majority of leading Western statesmen are seriously concerned with the problems of political and civic rights in the USSR or in China. In the final analysis, Nixon, Pompidou and Heath are defending the interests of the ruling classes of their own countries, and it should by no means be assumed that capitalist circles in the USA, Britain, France or Western Germany are particularly interested in a rapid development of socialist democracy in the USSR or in accelerating the pace of economic, social and cultural progress in our country.

Thus when Soviet dissidents appeal for support in the Western countries, they must know exactly to whom they are addressing their appeals. To us, it is obvious that public opinion in the Western countries is extraordinarily polarized and reacts in very different ways to events in the USSR and in the other socialist countries. In fact, those who are primarily interested in the development of a truly socialist democracy in our country are the left-wing forces of the West, in other words socialist and communist Parties, progressive intellectuals, and various leftist organizations. Right-wing circles in the West, on the contrary, exploit any shortcomings in the USSR and any acts of oppression by the Soviet State for their own demagogic ends; their aim is not to assist the victory of a 'socialism with a human face' but to discredit both socialism and communism, and thereby strike a blow above all against the forces of the Left in their own countries.

Certain of our dissidents sometimes give the impression that they fully understand this. They transfer their dissatisfaction with the political practice of the CPSU to the whole Left in the West, and consider that there too a victory of the Left would yield no more than a new variety of totalitarianism. In their declarations, addresses and protests these dissidents have lately more and more appealed not so much to the Left as to the Right in the Western countries. This orientation offers no hope for the future, although, of course, every Soviet citizen should be free to choose his own political convictions and sympathies.

Trade: An Example of the Limits of External Powers

It is well known that the 1972 grain harvest in the Soviet Union was very poor. Since no large cereal stocks are available in our country from previous years, there has been a serious dearth of grain for human and animal consumption. This shortage was, however, minimized by unprecedentedly large purchases from the USA, Canada, and a number of other countries. Large consignments of other commodities were also bought abroad. It can naturally be assumed that if Western businessmen and governmental agencies had refused to sell grain and other commodities to the USSR, grave supply difficulties would have arisen in our country in 1972-3. This would undoubtedly have increased discontent among the masses, which might have had to be allayed by some kind of political concessions. All this is, of course, mere hypothesis. In any case, it would have become necessary to adopt economic measures to ensure a swifter development of our agriculture. But why on that account would American producers have denied themselves a lucrative deal? From their point of view, why should they give up their profits?

To help to develop Soviet agriculture, or to convert the USSR within a short space of time from an importer of grain, meat, and butter into an exporter of these goods is not the aim of the US farm lobby. Of course, the ruling class in the USA may elect to break economic relations with any country, as it did with Cuba. The purpose of that decision was clear and the loss to US economy from the blockade of Cuba was insignificant. However, if this kind of boycott did not achieve its purpose in the case of Cuba, it would be even more senseless if applied to the USSR, at a time when the development of trade relations with the Soviet Union promises no small advantages to the West. Naturally, trade with the West strengthens the economic position of the USSR. However, the West of course also derives self-interested advantages from it. At present, the Western countries seek to import raw materials from the Soviet Union for their industries – iron ore, timber, oil and gas. The USSR also exports to the West and to Japan various metals and gold bullion. In their turn, the West and Japan export to the USSR various kinds of equipment – mainly, it would seem, for the oil, gas and timber industries, for coalmining and harbour installations – as well as light industrial goods, grains and foodstuffs. Significantly, the Jackson Amendment would make it difficult to import Soviet finished products into the USA, but it would in no way hamper either US exports of equipment or grain to the USSR or imports of Soviet raw materials to the USA. This merely demonstrates once again that the emergence of the USSR on the world market as a strong industrial power, exporting high quality machinery, light industrial products, motor cars or aircraft to the Western countries as well as to the less developed lands, is a prospect which is far from being the dream of Western businessmen.

There are also limits to the efficacy of external pressures from public organizations and press organs. The Western public rightly protests against attempts to deprive a man like Sakharov of the possibility of freely expressing his views, or a writer like Solzhenitsyn of the normal conditions required for literary creation, against the imprisonment of Amalrik or the confinement in psychiatric hospitals of men like Grigorenko, Plyushch and others. On the other hand, no one could insist that Sakharov's declarations or interviews be given fully sympathetic treatment in *Pravda* or *Izvestya,* or that Solzhenitsyn's new novels be praised in *Novy Mir* or *Znamya.* At the same time it cannot be regarded as normal that Soviet citizens should learn of dissidents' statements or artistic works only from foreign broadcasts and newspapers. We have already had occasion to propose that some institutional machinery should be set up in our country for a dialogue with the various dissenting groups.

The Dangers of Russo-Centrism

At present public opinion in the West reacts much more sharply and actively to negative events in the USSR than it did 15 or 35 years ago. Nevertheless, it would be an illusion to think that the Western public will become more preoccupied by the internal problems of the USSR than by those within their own countries. In this respect we do not consider that Solzhenitsyn's strictures in his address 'Peace and Violence' are just. However important external pressure, in the last analysis the fundamental problems of any country and especially of large powers such as the USSR, can only be resolved by the people and government of that country.

Solzhenitsyn writes: 'Could a Negro militant in South Africa be detained and tormented with impunity for four years as General Grigorenko has been? The storm of world indignation would have torn the roof off his prison long ago'. This position is mistaken. In the same address we find no such strong words of protest, of which Solzhenitsyn is so capable, against the odious apartheid system in South Africa. Unfortunately, no protests have yet torn the roofs off the prisons and camps where hundreds of thousands of South

African blacks are incarcerated. No protests have yet flung open the
gates of the concentration camps in Indonesia where hundreds of
thousands are held without trial for their left-wing beliefs. No
protests have yet halted the bloody terror in Chile. Of course, one's
own pain always seems worse than that of others. Nevertheless,
it is impermissible to fall into a kind of 'Moscow-Centrism' and fail
to see that in many other countries there are political problems just
as acute and very often even more acute than those of the USSR.

The Short-term and Long-term Prospects for Détente

Global international détente, just as the lessening of tension in any
area of the world, depends on the governments and leaders in power
at this particular time. It is evident that at present the Soviet government is greatly interested in relaxing international confrontation and
developing external co-operation and trade. To achieve these aims it
is prepared to make certain concessions which it would not have
contemplated a few years ago. The major Western countries are also
prepared to make many concessions. Nevertheless, in neither case
should important concessions on internal policy be expected. It
would therefore be unrealistic and wrong for the West to deliver
any ultimatum that the USSR should fulfil certain preconditions for
diplomatic détente and economic co-operation. We believe that
détente, co-operation, trade, and tourism are important benefits in
themselves. More often than not, it is unreasonable to pose preconditions in negotiating these questions. For it is surely plain that in
the past the high pitch of international tension drained the strength
of the great powers by a futile arms race, and diverted their enormous resources away from the development of their productive potential into the accumulation of unprecedented means of destruction.

Hitherto the détente has not led to any enlargement of democratic
liberties in the USSR; on the contrary, it has been used by certain
groups to tighten suppression of dissent. However, in a more distant
future – although this may not be a very comforting prognosis –
détente will undoubtedly contribute to the extension of democratic
rights and liberties in our country. For it is precisely in periods of
détente that the efficacy of public opinion grows considerably in
shaping the internal affairs of each major power. By contrast, a
country which is isolated and cut off from the outside world by
various Cold War barriers becomes insensitive to protests and views

beyond its frontiers. We can see the truth of this not only in the case of great powers, but even in the case of little Albania. In this sense, it must be said that the relaxation of international tension is in itself a very important pre-condition, though not the only one, for the development of democracy in Soviet society. For this reason, we believe that Brandt was justified to state that he would advocate détente even if Stalin were still in power.

In conclusion, we would repeat that no matter how significant the pressure of progressive international opinion may be, the prime impulse towards democratization in the USSR must necessarily come from within Soviet society itself, including its present and future leaders. The present regressive trends in our domestic political life are, of course, a disquieting symptom. But they do not in any way preclude the emergence of other trends and other situations, whose outlines are difficult to foresee now. During the last fifteen to twenty years a new generation has grown up in the USSR and with it a new levy of leaders, a significant number of whom may prove capable of an outlook on the problems and prospects of development that differs from that of the leaders of the outgoing generation.

It is clear that a majority of our leaders now increasingly understands that it is intolerable that the Soviet Union should lag so far behind the capitalist countries in the *material living standards* of its population. — the production of the basic necessities of life for our people. Some effective steps have already been taken to remedy this. But the level of our production of spiritual values is extremely low, although the majority of Soviet people precisely regards spiritual nourishment as an ever more important component of their needs. At the same time it is obvious that without true democracy, without a free exchange of ideas and opinions, it is absolutely impossible to create any satisfactory spiritual values. Let us hope that in time all Soviet people, including the majority of their leaders, will make this simple truth their own.

November 1973

2: Dissent and Free Discussion

I have been reproached for initiating among the "dissidents" a discussion that is supposedly inadmissible "for moral reasons". "There are too few of us," one of my friends wrote to me. "We are all under such strong pressure from the authorities that we cannot allow ourselves the luxury of open discussion."

I cannot agree with this point of view.

The democratic movement in the USSR has never been united, and the polemic within it has been going on for a long time. It is clear that we must all stand together when it comes to speaking out in defence of civil rights and protesting against tyranny and violations of legality. However, the ideas different groups of dissenters have on ways and means for — and mainly on the goals and the character of — the democratization necessary for our country, differ in many respects. Therefore, discussion on all these questions is inevitable and useful.

"The details of political views are truly immaterial at the present time," says one of the letters I received. But, in reality, what is involved is not details, but principles. A.I. Solzhenitsyn's "Letter to the Rulers of the Soviet Union", published recently in the West, bears witness to this. This document caused profound disappointment among the majority of people who sincerely respect Solzhenitsyn for his artistic talent and courage. But of course, personal respect for a man who is openly and uncompromisingly fighting against tyranny and violence cannot and *must not* compel people to be silent when they do not agree with the great writer's retrograde views on the history of Russia and perspectives for Russia's development and on the democratic institutions of the West. And it has long been known that truth is not born from the reverent memorization of the words of a "Great Teacher" (even if he is not persecuting but is being persecuted). Truth arises only out of a clash of ideas and through arguments. Therefore, we who seek truth should not impose in our midst a mechanism whereby we must "copy" one another or prohibit ourselves from arguing.

"A major discussion among the dissidents," wrote V. Chalidze in his 'Open Letter', is no less valuable than the existence of dissent itself." I agree with this.

On pressure "from below" and concessions "from above"

In my article, I wrote about the mounting dissatisfaction and discontent among the broad masses of our people with many aspects of Soviet life. I contended, however, that given the obvious political passivity of the people, pressure from below is very, very weakly felt by "the top" and, therefore, cannot lead to rapid changes in the direction of democratization.

"You do not know our working class and peasantry," argue two Old Bolsheviks. "Our people are at present exhibiting a very high level of activity. Look at what kind of counterplans they are advancing in the factories and how socialist competition has been developed here. Many important initiatives are coming from the village. The problem is simply that we, the intelligentsia, are not yet able to take advantage of this mounting activity among the people and cannot direct it toward the struggle against bureaucratism and for the democratization of society."

"Roy Medvedev is an armchair scientist," D. Panin writes in an article published in several emigré newspapers. "He has spent his life studying books published mainly in the USSR. Hence his total lack of information. The population of the USSR has carried on and is carrying on year after year a continuous smoldering struggle against the hated régime of enslavement using the means available to them very effectively . . . Roy Medvedev's statement about the political passivity of the workers and peasants does not correspond to reality. The rank-and-file toilers in the grip of terror do not appear openly signing, shall we say petitions, for example, but apply more effective means. They carry on a clandestine economic struggle." According to Panin's words, it is precisely this conscious economic sabotage by the people that not only explains the economic and technical difficulties of the USSR, but will lead, it seems, in the not too distant future to an "explosion of the system from within", the "overthrow of the class of party bureaucrats", and the "collapse of the ideology of Marxism-Leninism", which is in principle incompatible with democracy.

"Our government fully and organically fits our people," says one of the 'Open Letters' I received. "Look at the people around you. The majority of them need nothing. They have a television, vodka, a few diversions, and they are totally satisfied. These people do not need any sort of democratization. The present generation of the Russian nation and intelligentsia only proves the correctness of the saying that every people deserves the government it has.".

It goes without saying, I do not pretend to have a profound knowledge of the thoughts and moods of all layers of our people, a scientific study of which is not generally conducted here — in any case, not openly. But I also do not believe I am especially ignorant in this respect. And I do not believe any of the points of view cited above to be correct.

Of course, everywhere in our country there are people who are doing excellent work with enthusiasm in their areas, be it smelting steel, testing lasers, cultivating grain, or raising children. But people who love their work are everywhere. This is in no way a sign of political activism.

But just as mistaken is the conception of some sort of "smolder-ing and clandestine" economic struggle with a deliberate reduction of labour productivity, worsening of the quality of goods, and so on. And although dissatisfaction with many aspects of Soviet reality exists, on the whole the population of the country — even if only deep down and passively — supports the principal aspects of the foreign and domestic policy of the ruling circles.

Undoubtedly, this is explained to a large degree by the fact that they are misinformed. The state of affairs within the country and abroad is presented to the majority of our people in a distorted light. The most obvious example: August 1968, when the entry of Soviet troops into the territory of the Czechoslovak Soviet Socialist Repub-lic did not meet any objections from the overwhelming majority of our people. As a rule, the ordinary people in our country believed the version of events propagated by the Soviet press — that an in-vasion of Czechoslovakia was being prepared by the GFR [Federal Republic of Germany] or NATO forces, that a counter-revolutionary overturn in a fraternal socialist country was imminent, and so on. The officers and soldiers sent into the Czechoslovak SSR from the Soviet military divisions were prepared to shoot these imaginary counter-revolutionaries. These soldiers and officers, upon receiving the order, would have advanced into the territory of any other country — for example, into the Near East — in the same efficient and disciplined manner. This is because even in such critical situations, we have practically no pressure from below when there is no crystallized public opinion. In any case, it is not a factor that the government must pay attention to.

For the time being, we have no *mass* movement, either openly or covertly, for the democratization of the country, much less a mass struggle for a change in the economic, social, and political system in the USSR. And it is difficult to anticipate how strong pressure "from below" in defence of democratic freedoms will be in the coming years. But what is involved here is in no way some peculiar feature of the Russian nation and the Russian intelligentsia.

Russia, as is well known, rushed through the stage of bourgeois-democratic revolution in several months. These several months, in the course of which Russia was — according to Lenin's expression — the freest country in the world, was not enough time for any sort of stable democratic traditions to come into being in the country or to consolidate in the people's consciousness convictions as to the enormous value of such democratic freedoms as the freedom of assembly and organization.

One must remember, besides, that the population of the USSR in its majority did not yet pass through a period of being saturated with basic material wealth, after which follows, as a rule, a clearer awareness of a short supply of spiritual nourishment, civil rights, and freedom as well as the demand to take part in the making of fundamental decisions concerning the life of the people and management of local affairs and production. It is not surprising that people are more indifferent to a shortage of democratic freedoms than they are to a shortage of meat and milk. It is natural that people react first of all to a shortage of those goods that they have already become accustomed to having.

All this, however, does not give anyone the moral right to contemptuously condemn the people instead of trying to bring home to them the indissoluble link between the democratization of the system of government and an improvement of the people's living standard. A lack of understanding of this link and an indifference to the problems of democratization are explained not by any peculiar attributes of the Russian people but by the historical route our country has gone through. That is why the pressure from below is so insignificant in our country and why the demands for a renewal of our ideological and political institutions and for the establishment of genuine socialist democracy sound so weak. The weakness of pressure from below is especially striking when compared with the mounting administrative, ideological, and political pressure from the top directed toward the suppression of intellectual freedom, an even greater homogeneity of thought among the Soviet people, and the propagation of antiquated ideological dogmas and norms that more often than not have nothing in common with Marxism.

The political passivity of the broad masses is a sad but real fact that we cannot help but take into account in our discussions and prognoses. But I never believed that democratic freedoms could only be granted to us "from above" and that it was therefore necessary to fold up the democratic movement and wait for favours from the government. My thinking, perhaps poorly expressed, was that the expansion of the democratic movement, which unfortunately until now has been primarily the concern of individuals or small groups of intellectuals, will increase the chances for definite concessions from above; and this in turn will multiply the forms of the democratic movement and facilitate its activity.

However, some of my opponents do not want to hear about this interrelationship between pressure from below and concessions from above. "If it must come from above, then I don't need such democratization," one of them declared not long ago. But here one must say frankly that if we do not intend to call for revolutionary means or dream about some sort of coup d'état, we can count only on pressure from below and — as a result of it — on concessions from above.

Of course, that which is given from above is comparatively easily taken back. The "liberalization" of the beginning of the 1960s and the reinstitution of a harsher course at the end of the 1960s was clear enough evidence of this. Only the presence of stable democratic traditions within the society can guarantee against such turns. But these traditions do not arise by themselves. They are built and consolidated only in the course of a mass political movement that cannot be simply a spontaneous movement. Such a movement demands the establishment of organizations, the advancement of leaders, the elaboration of different political conceptions, the struggle of opinions, and so forth. But all this can only emerge given the presence of a certain openness to express views and a certain minimum of democratic freedoms that do not exist now and which the democratic movement must secure. To assert that concessions from above are impossible in principle, to repudiate even the very minimal reforms that offer a potential for improving the political climate in our country — such an orientation is unrealistic: it virtually closes off the most realistic course for the democratization of our society.

A few words on the infrastructure of present-day Soviet society

Soviet society as it is at the present time is a peculiar and still very-little-studied phenomenon. The fundamental features and mechanisms for the functioning of our political and social organism are not sufficiently clear even to those who are at the top of the "pyramid". Hence, apparently, the shortcomings in their reactions to the most negligible manifestations of dissent and the pettiness that so often surprises foreign observers.

The undemocratic nature of the present political structure in the USSR is obvious and it is not difficult to outline the democratic reforms desired for our country. The implementations of such reforms, harmoniously combining socialism and democracy, would undoubtedly enrich our people both materially and spiritually and would make socialism incomparably more attractive to the peoples of all the world. But *how*, in the conditions we have, do we pave the way for such reforms?

Academician A.D. Sakharov considers his positions and demands as "purely moral". It is of considerable importance to declare moral demands, and this is natural for a learned physicist. But for people devoting themselves professionally to the political and social sciences moral indignation alone is not enough. While studying Soviet society, they must seek realistic possibilities and realistic routes for its democratic development.

From a purely moral position, one can, of course, not just hold "the elite" accountable for their actions but can also reproach the intelligentsia, if only for its political passivity. However, if we want not only to declare our feelings but also to secure real changes, we must proceed from the real state of things. In our conclusions and calculations we thus must bear in mind *this* people, *this* youth, *this* intelligentsia, *this* ruling elite, and *this* régime, which will not be routed by statements and books but which can (although this task is extremely difficult) be gradually transformed to secure the establishment of socialism "with a human face". For this to happen, of course, we need a better knowledge of *what it is* we want to change.

In the democratic countries of the West with their relative freedom of speech and press and the large number of different organizations, from the extreme right to the extreme left, the links between society and the state apparatus are very complex and indirect. The social infrastructure there is in many ways independent of the state. In addition, private ownership of a large part of the means of production, the firms in the service industries, and the mass media is not just a means of exploiting people; it does not just produce anarchy and disregard of the public interest. By meeting certain social needs, private production creates to a certain extent a self-regulating economic system. This not only relieves the state organs of many responsibilities but weakens their influence on public affairs. On the other hand, privately owned companies, while making good use of the state, remain in many respects independent of it. Thus, for example, while fully controlling the official activities of their employees, making their material well-being dependent upon their loyalty to the interests of the firm, these firms and monopolies are more or less indifferent to the nationality and the religious and political persuasions of their employees; at any rate, they have the option of being indifferent.

Soviet society does not have such a complex infrastructure at the present time. Of course, in the USSR, too, there are different social layers and groups with diverse interests that often do not coincide with one another, and there are people with different views. However, all these differences are hardly manifested at all in the system of social relations. Given the one-party system; the absence of genuine self-government in enterprises and municipal organs; and the absence of independent newspapers, journals, and publishers, almost the entire economic and social life of our huge country is run from a single centre. All social organizations, including even some sort of society for cactus, canary, or dog fanciers, are not independent but work under the control of corresponding organizations of the CPSU. The work of all the organs of the press and all publishing houses is controlled particularly closely.

The party and state organs are responsible for the work of the largest enterprises and the smallest repair shops, the huge restaurants and the tiniest snackbar. They look after the construction of new cities and after the work on elevators and waterpipes in each individual home. The party organizations, like a nervous system, penetrate into every cell of our social organism, while the state organs make up what could be considered its bone and muscle system. The entire system for maintaining the life of the Soviet people is dependent upon the activity of party and state officials, and they time and again make every citizen in the USSR concretely aware of this.

Such a cumbersome and unyielding structure of rule, devoid of any sort of democratic counterweight, undoubtedly serves as an obstacle to the economic, intellectual, and moral development of society. The tendency toward bureaucratization in the party and state organs is becoming almost insurmountable. Poor work by any institution of leadership has an extremely unhealthy effect on the entire social organism. In addition, the struggles – independent of social control – flaring up from time to time between different departments and individual leaders (arising more often than not around administrative interests or simply personal flaws rather than motives of principle) inflict tremendous material and moral damage upon the society.

Such a system can turn out to be extremely vulnerable given the emergence of some type of internal crisis, as we have seen to one degree or another in the examples of Hungary, Poland, and Czechoslovakia. Nevertheless, this inflexible, and in a certain sense even fragile, structure is extremely powerful. The social infrastructure that has taken shape in our country gives the leadership of the party and state a degree of power and opportunities for manipulation and control heretofore unparalleled in any society. This is precisely why it is difficult to expect any rapid and radical changes in our country.

What then remains? The course of slow and gradual evolutionary change remains the most realistic. Despite the growing pressure from above, the democratic opposition of all shades must secure the extension of freedom of speech and organization and the development of social control, i.e., the establishment of the democratic counterweights indispensable for society. Any initiative in this direction deserves attention. It is impermissible to let even the smallest chance slip by.

It is necessary to see clearly that the fear experienced by a majority of the party leaders and ideologues at the thought of a possible democratization has by no means been produced by a concern for the preservation of Marxism and socialism. If one realistically assesses what exists, it is not difficult to demonstrate that the realization of even the most maximum demands of today's democratic movement (for example, on the creation of social and political organizations and organs of the press independent of the CPSU) would lead neither to the collapse of Marxism nor to the renunciation of the leading role of the CPSU, as our ideologues so fear and as the opponents of Marxism so fervently hope. On the contrary, it would make possible the cleansing and purification of the party and its ideology; a rejuvenation of its leadership; the lessening of bureaucratism in its apparatus; and, in the end, the development and enrichment of Marxism to make it conform to the conditions existing at the end of the twentieth century. A much greater danger for the USSR and for socialism as a whole emanates from retaining and deepening the violations of democracy that we have observed in our country in recent years.

On pressure from outside

While not too much concerned with the public opinion that is only just coming into being within the country, the Soviet leadership is much more sensitive to criticism from outside. For many reasons the political leaders of the USSR are interested today in good relations not only with the governments of the Western countries but with the social circles of these countries that exert influence on the policies of their governments. Therefore, critical statements from Western society against violations of civil rights in the USSR have great importance; in some instances they exert a pressure that the internal democratic movement is as yet incapable of exercising.

I wrote about this in my article, emphasizing that the support of left-wing, progressive circles of Western society is especially valuable for us. This does not at all mean that the leadership of the USSR is not sensitive to criticism from other influential social forces of East and West. Nevertheless, for the participants in the struggle for civil rights in the USSR, it is most natural to appeal for support to representatives of those social forces that in their own countries act in defence of civil rights. It is difficult to believe in the sincerity of support for Soviet "dissidents" from the Chinese or Spanish press or from the extreme right-wing circles of the West which serve as obstacles to the expansion of social, economic, and civil rights in their own countries.

Many different types of influences from the public in the Western countries are exerted also on the positions of the political leaders of these countries — our partners in negotiations. In the end, any talks in our time are inconceivable without mutual pressure and also without mutual concessions. These talks reflect not only the serious conflicts between the different countries but the presence of some kind of minimal good will. Therefore, the mutual demands from the parties involved must originate from the real relationship of forces and must not take on the character of an ultimatum. And here it is appropriate to say a few words again on Senator Jackson's celebrated amendment.

Democratization and Detente

The refusal of the USA to trade with Cuba expresses very clearly the United States' disapproval of the Cuban régime and creates serious difficulties for the latter. However, a position like this on the part of the USA is not, strictly speaking, interference in the internal affairs of Cuba. Every country decides for itself with whom it will maintain economic and political relations and to what extent. The USSR does not extend credits to either Greece or Portugal, but this also is not interference in the internal affairs of those countries.

From this point of view, one can understand the feelings of those US congressmen who speak out against granting the USSR American credits and most-favoured-nation status. These people are accustomed to viewing the USSR as an ideological and political opponent of the USA, and they fear a growth of our economic potential resulting from our access to Western credits and technology. Moreover, the grievances of American legislators over the absence of freedom of emigration from the USSR are totally valid.

However, the number of such grievances can be very large, and if they are set forth in the form of obligatory preliminary terms, no real progress toward improving international relations will be possible. This was shown by the recent amendment of Senator Buckley demanding that neither credits nor most-favoured-nation status be extended to the USSR until our country stops jamming the broadcasts of Radio Liberty.

Moreover, it is fully possible to lodge similar grievances against many Western countries, including the USA, where problems of civil and economic rights are being handled in ways that are far from always satisfactory, as one can see from the speeches of many American congressmen. Even in a country that takes pride in its centuries-old democratic traditions, like Switzerland, women did not have the right to vote until very recently and were not represented either in unions or in the cantonal parliaments. Until the present time, however, this has not interfered with Switzerland's foreign trade.

It is necessary to take into account other important considerations as well. Not long ago the oil crisis clearly showed how vulnerable the West European countries and Japan are to economic pressure. The position of the USSR in this respect is far more stable. Trade with the USA and American credits very much interest the leadership in the USSR. However, this interest is not so great that the government of the Soviet Union would move toward a change in domestic legislation or toward any essential alteration of its internal policy. This is especially true since other Western countries and Japan, whose economic situations are not so stable as that of the USA, have been manifesting in recent years an ever-growing readiness for economic collaboration with the USSR.

In his article already referred to above, D. Panin, who not long ago left the USSR, tries to demonstrate that the material situation of the Soviet people is steadily deteriorating. Therefore, Panin calls on the West to stop granting economic aid and credits to Moscow because this supposedly postpones "the internal explosion and liberation of peoples". But this is obviously erroneous. In the Soviet Union a noticeable expansion of the production of consumer goods and services is taking place. One of the main factors motivating the majority of Soviet people today is the desire to improve their living standard, and this can be achieved fundamentally only by increasing production and the productivity of labour.

The absence of credits and economic aid from the West will not halt economic progress in our country and improvements in our people's well-being; these processes would in this case only be slowed down. The real hope for the democratization of Soviet society can only be linked with scientific-technological and economic progress, the interests of which come into conflict with our unwieldy bureaucratic administrative structure.

Therefore, the slogan "The worse it is, the better" that Panin and his co-thinkers have advanced is absolutely inadmissible for those who actually want the best for the Soviet people and for all their neighbours on the planet.

The process of changing internal régimes, especially in the greatest countries of the world, unfortunately proceeds at a slow and often very agonizing pace. The expansion of international trade and international division of labour based on mutual concessions can hasten this process somewhat. But it is impossible to hasten it by ultimatums or by refusing to make compromises. Even a real threat of atomic annihilation will not force the USA to abandon today its exceedingly outmoded domestic institutions, which, under the pressure of the progress taking place in this country, will in time be eliminated by the American people themselves.

Meanwhile, a confrontation of the great powers, fraught with the danger of the destruction of all humanity, has in the last ten years entered into a critical phase. The arms race will do colossal economic damage to people of all countries, no less than has been the case in the recent past. To save ourselves from or even minimize the damage is possible only through joint efforts. There is no other way.

The tremendous importance of the task of preserving the earth's biosphere also cannot be decided within the boundaries of individual countries or continents. It can only be resolved by joint efforts. Therefore, the course proposed by Solzhenitsyn for Russian national self-isolation and the "policy of isolated salvation amid the general confusion" can end up being no less destructive than the policy of mutual confrontation and competition. One example alone will suffice: the contamination of the upper layers of the atmosphere by certain harmful wastes can by the twenty-first century destroy the present structure of the troposphere and stratosphere, which will lead to a sharp increase in ultraviolet radiation and destruction of all the vegetation on our planet, including that in Siberia — in the development of which Solzhenitsyn sees Russia's salvation.

Competition of the great powers in the delivery of arms to the countries of Africa and Latin America cannot be tolerated. But it is just as intolerable for industrially developed countries "to leave South America to its own devices" or "to let Africa find out for itself how to begin an independent course of state and civilization", as Solzhenitsyn proposed. In the contemporary world it is impossible to save oneself alone.

A little more than a year ago the GDR [German Democratic Republic] was not invited to the United Nations' world conference on the protection of the environment convened in Stockholm. This country had not yet joined any of the United Nations' specialized organizations. This was an example of how immediate and insignificant political aims of a few states have prevailed over the long-term interests of humanity. Unfortunately, the reaction of the USSR was just as mistaken: not limiting itself to a resolute protest the Soviet Union altogether refused to take part in the Stockholm conference. If solving other problems concerning all humanity becomes dependent upon narrow political problems of the moment, very bad times await our planet.

The development of affairs in our world creates, nevertheless, the objective necessity for collaboration and compromise, first of all, among the great powers. Such collaboration does not exclude either ideological struggle or different forms of ideological pressure. However, in utilizing this pressure, it is always necessary to stay within intelligent limits which if exceeded could again give rise to an uncontrolled and destructive escalation of distrust and competition. This is why Brandt's logic seems to us, all things considered, preferable to Strauss's logic; and why Kissinger's logic is preferable to the logic of Senators Jackson and Buckley.

April 1974

3: Watergate: A View from
the Soviet Union

Richard Nixon and his policy

Ten or 11 years ago I learned from the radio station *The Voice of America* about Richard Nixon's visit to West Berlin, which was then experiencing difficult times. It looked as if Nixon, a former vice-president defeated in the Presidential elections as well as in the elections to the governorship of California, was about to disappear for ever from the political scene. He had been connected with many events of the cold war and with McCarthyism, and he had deservedly won his reputation as an extreme right-winger of the Republican camp. Not only the Soviet, but also the American liberal press, made fun of his political failures. His visit to Berlin would have scarcely attracted the attention of the mass media, if it were not for one incident.

The Voice of America mentioned that one night Nixon somehow got himself across the "Berlin Wall" and went for a walk in East Berlin. During that walk he approached some passers-by, engaging them in conversation and asking all sorts of questions on most delicate topics. After that he crossed the Wall again and returned to West Berlin.

I well remember that at the time this whole incident seemed to me a complete invention. If, however, this night stroll really did take place, then it made the impression of a cheap publicity stunt, much below the dignity of a great statesman, an aspirant to the highest office of the United States. Generally speaking, most of what the American press wrote about Nixon did not arouse any sympathy for the man, who was presented as a dull-witted adventurer and political trickster.

I was sure that the unexpected victory of Nixon in 1968 over his party's more liberal candidate, Senator Nelson Rockefeller, and later over the Democratic Senator Vice-President Hubert Humphrey was not so much connected with Nixon's "new look" as with the growing tension in international relations: and particularly with Soviet intervention in Czechoslovakia. The Soviet Union had embarked on a tougher course in its foreign policy and the West retorted by bringing to the fore tougher people considered to be more actively anti-communist. This was an interpretation shared also by many Western newspapers. In one Western paper I saw, in September 1968, a cartoon of Nixon engaged in a telephone conversation with Brezhnev: "The entry of your troops to Prague helped considerably in my electoral campaign. But you could do even more for me if you occupied Rumania and Yugoslavia too."

However, the revision of American foreign policy, undertaken by the newly elected President, was an obvious departure from the traditions of the cold war; and this attracted the attention of the whole world. Right from the beginning, Nixon declared that he would endeavour to limit the arms race and to achieve detente; that he would seek an honourable peace in Vietnam; and that in the relations between the great powers it was time to go over from confrontation to negotiations. These were not empty words.

True, Nixon was not consistent in his policy. In 1970 he could not resist the temptation to try and solve the Vietnam crisis by armed contest. It was Nixon who ordered American troops to invade Cambodia and to support Thieu in his attempt to cut the Ho Chi Minh Trail in Laos. However, a quick defeat of the whole enterprise and energetic protests in the United States forced Nixon back onto the road of negotiations and compromises. In the end, precisely Nixon and Kissinger were able to bring to a speedy conclusion the talks in Paris and to withdraw all American troops from Vietnam, Laos, and Cambodia, without too much loss of face. And though the military conflict in the Indochinese Peninsula still goes on, it remains to a certain degree localized and does not present the same danger to world peace as it used to some time ago.

The man who had the reputation of a fierce anti-communist, managed to achieve a radical change in the relations between the United States and China, a change which resulted in the re-admission of one of the largest countries to the United Nations and to the Security Council. However one evaluates the motives which induced Nixon and Mao to conclude an agreement, one should not dismiss the fact that the normalization of relations between China and the USA and the return of China to the United Nations will have a restraining influence on the foreign policy of the Chinese leaders.

The man, who never before concealed his anti-Soviet views, not only paid a visit to the USSR, but was able to adopt a policy of good will and cooperation, and of negotiations on a wide range of most important problems. Of course, the change from confrontation to negotiations was not easy for the Soviet leaders. But for the American Administration these first steps were even more difficult and Nixon's personal role was significant.

Already pushed to the wall by his political opponents, Nixon — with Kissinger's help (or Kissinger with Nixon's help) — was able to reach a compromise in the Middle East and to persuade the warring parties — with the USA as mediator — to accept this compromise. This led to a remarkable change in Arab-American relations without damage to the relations between the United States and Israel.

All in all, the successes of American foreign policy under Nixon were quite considerable; and Senator Humphrey could hardly, within the same period of time, have achieved such results.

Some lessons of Watergate

In the new President there remained, however, quite a great deal of the old Nixon — remote, secretive, inclined to engage in all manner of behind-the-scenes machinations and political intrigues. It was hard to believe that the attempts at installing bugging equipment in the headquarters of the Democratic Party at Watergate was made at the initiative of some unimportant subordinate officials. It was even more difficult to believe that Nixon's accomplices tried to hush up the scandal and to exert pressure on the judiciary without the President's knowledge. And it would have been difficult, even impossible, to prove Nixon's complicity in this affair if he himself had not before made use of bugging devices and if he had not been recording all his confidential conversations on tapes. It is quite believable that he planned to use these tape recordings at some future date in writing his memoirs. However, he received the opportunity to do this well in advance of the end of his Presidential term. Nixon's efforts to avoid surrendering the tapes, the long and ugly story of his struggle with the judicial investigators and with the Commission of the Congress, the publication of his own version of the recorded talks, the disappearance of some tapes, the refusal to hand over the most important recordings, and so on — all this led to protracted investigation; it also created a crisis of leadership, contributed to the unsettling of the whole of American society, and undermined the Americans' confidence in their President. Of course, even statesmen on a lower level of the administrative hierarchy have the right to engage in confidential talks with their private assistants. But such talks are not usually recorded by officials expressly assigned to the job. And what kind of independent court, investigating a criminal case, would put the right of a politician to confidentiality above the consideration of the law once the existence of such tangible evidence becomes publicly known? Not every assistant would be likely to agree to serve a long prison sentence instead of his boss. It became clear that Nixon's dismissal or impeachment was inevitable when the American Supreme Court, as it was expected, reached its decision unanimously.

In his article "Peace and Violence", A. Solzhenitsyn sneers at the "noisy Watergate affair", at the "distorted views" of the Senate leaders and the "great hypocrisy" of American political life. "The fury of the Democrats in connection with Watergate" looks to Solzhenitsyn like a "parody of the furious and rash assault on the Cadets against Goremykin-Sturmer in 1915-1916".[1] (The Cadets' criticism of the incorrect way the Tsarist authorities were conducting military operations facilitated the abolition of Russian absolutism). It is difficult to agree with such an attitude on the part of our leading writer. It seem to us that the Watergate affair, which ended with the dismissal of Nixon and with the bringing of many of his officials and assistants to justice, will contribute to the cleansing of American political life and to the growth of the sense of responsibility of American leaders and of the whole nation. The outcome of this affair revealed not only the weaknesses but also a great deal of soundness in American constitutional democracy, as well as the important role of wide and open dissemination of information.

Solzhenitsyn refers to "mutual deceptions and to abuses during the previous presidential campaign". It is true that abuses were not infrequent. Unfortunately, the main culprits usually went undetected: they left no trace of their misdeeds, therefore those who were caught became the scapegoats. But in the Watergate affair the trail of lawlessness led all too obviously to the White House. Proud of his electronics, Nixon himself made of his own person a scapegoat, giving his political opponents on the left as well as on the right a tremendous chance to corner him.

It would not be proper to consider the Watergate affair only as a victory of American democracy, of freedom of the press, a victory of journalists over the President. One can assume that not all the attacks on Nixon were disinterested. It is possible that opponents of detente as well as known reactionaries and some lobbyists for the war industry also gave a helping hand to push him over. But all this could not possibly serve society as a pretext for not noticing such obvious abuses of power in its midst.

Calling the stormy debates that agitated the Americans for a considerable time "a thieves' quarrel", Solzhenitsyn appeals to western observers to give their "full attention" to what goes on in the Soviet Union because such events "do not simply take place in one country" but represent "the very morrow of mankind".

Soviet leaders and the Watergate affair

For the rank and file reader of the Soviet press all the changes of the American scene are not easy to understand. Commenting favourably on many aspects of Nixon's foreign policy and his recent visit to the USSR, our newspapers wrote practically nothing about Watergate, publishing from time to time only Nixon's own statements or those of his assistants and defenders. Our propaganda was not in a hurry to exploit the looming scandal in order to expose the contempt for law so prevalent at the very top of the bourgeois state machine. And this was not accidental.

At the time when the whole of the United States could hear on the radio and on television the statements of Nixon's opponents in the Congress, the Soviet press kept silent, and in this way expressed its support. The Soviet leaders continued to show not only their confidence in Nixon but their friendliness, promoting his thesis that precisely "personal relations" established between him and Brezhnev were helping detente and guaranteeing its development.

But the attitude of Soviet politicians can be explained not only by their preoccupation with the dangers which might threaten the policy of detente; the Watergate affair also irritated them because it demonstrated the important role of an opposition, of elected representatives vested with full powers, and the importance of an independent press and an independent judiciary in the control over the activities of executive bodies. Obviously, the initial event which led to the protracted campaign against the President and his high officials seemed to Nixon's Soviet partners completely unimportant and slight. In 1973 our hierarchy was of the opinion that this was an insignificant incident blown up by the opposition and that the whole outcry would soon die down. In a conversation with Academician Sakharov the deputy Procurator General of the USSR, M.P. Malyarov, called the Watergate affair "a demagogic trick". "All this is meant just as a show," declared Malyarov, "it will end in nothing if only Nixon shows determination. That's their democracy — just a hocus-pocus."

In our country there is no need to eavesdrop on the headquarters of the opposition party: oppositional organisations are banned. In elections, in any constituency, the voting paper bears the name of one candidate only. As to the numerous citizens with oppositional views, many of them are convinced that not only their telephones are tapped but that their flats are bugged as well. That is why more important discussions are conducted either in whispers or through written notes. And no newspapers would undertake to investigate whether such suspicions were groundless or not.

Some people, with whom I discussed the Watergate affair, were struck by the primitive manner in which "the job" was performed, for instance, the burglary at the house of Daniel Ellsberg's psychiatrist. It seemed incomprehensible that Nixon's important assistants and ministers turned to hired men when Nixon had at his disposal such specialized organizations as the FBI and the CIA. And how could examining magistrates, appointed by Nixon or belonging to his administration, investigate the activities of Nixon himself and of his entourage?

According to the general opinion, in our country the surveillance of known critics of the régime is done by competent bodies on a high professional level. And the militia will hardly get involved or even listen to a citizen complaining that he suspects that his home is bugged. At best they will advise him to rid himself of his "persecution mania".

In the USSR the interference of important officials or party leaders in the activities of juridical investigating authorities (in cases other than simple bribery of judges) is not regarded as an offence. Everybody knows that the search or the arrest of a functionary belonging to the regional or district "nomenklatura"[2] cannot be effected without previous consent from the regional or district office of the Party. It was not a secret that in Georgia, for instance, the Prosecutor General of the Republic endeavoured, for a long time and in vain, to obtain permission to interrogate and search members of the family of the former secretary of the Central Committee, V.P. Mzhavanadze. There was more than enough incriminating evidence, but the necessary permission to conduct an investigation was not obtained. Many stories circulate in the Ukraine, not only about the rudeness and harshness of the Politbureau member P. Shelest, but also about his abuses of power. But neither the judge, nor the Prosecutor of the Republic have examined the matter.

Fortunately, the time is over when not only an ordinary citizen but even any member of the Central Committee or the Politbureau (except Stalin) could be arrested and shot without any trial or investigation. Yet, it is difficult to make peace with a system under which the Soviet Establishment is securely protected not only from false accusations but also from any legitimate investigation into concrete examples of arbitrariness.

The end of Nixon and the perspectives of detente

Richard Nixon was dismissed and Gerald Ford took over. Wnat can the world expect from the new President? Will not the previous line of American foreign policy be abandoned as a personal contrivance of the compromised Nixon? So far such a conclusion seems unwarranted. It cannot even be ruled out that Ford will be able to achieve that in which his predecessor failed, having in the end spoiled his relations with Congress and with the press.

Obviously, there are, in the USA, not a few influential opponents of detente. There are active ultra-right and reactionary groups and leaders who are frightened of any cooperation with the USSR, viewing it only as an aggressive communist state which aims at imposing its own power upon the whole world, and in the first instance, at destroying the American system and the American way of life. Such people are afraid that detente and cooperation with the Soviet Union will contribute to the spread of abhorrent socialist and communist ideas and movements in the United States. American ultra-right circles would welcome the destruction or disintegration of the Soviet Union, but as this is impossible to achieve, they are ready to separate themselves from the USSR by an iron curtain.

But we also have similar reactionaries (though they consider themselves communists) who are afraid of the development of detente and of cooperation with the West. They are afraid that together with commodities and machinery, together with tourists and scientists, there will also arrive western ideas and views. They are afraid that the Soviet people will receive, as a result of detente, not only material goods but also a new outlook on reality, an outlook which differs from many myths of our present day propaganda. Such dogmatists and reactionaries see the United States only as an aggressive imperialist State, which aims at imposing its own power on the whole world and, in the first instance, at destroying the Soviet way of life. They would welcome the destruction or economic collapse of the United States, but as this is impossible, they too are ready to separate themselves from the USA and from Western Europe by an iron curtain.

Incidentally, these fears of the reactionaries and the conservatives are not quite without foundation, if one takes into account their very own interests. It is much more difficult for such people, in the West and in the East, to exist and to impose their will on others in an atmosphere of detente than in the conditions of cold war. The sooner they lose their influence, the better it will be both for the USSR and the USA.

In the West the extreme radicals also raise their voices against peaceful coexistence and detente. It seems to them that an atmosphere of cooperation weakens revolutionary consciousness and slows down progress in the West. Detente, according to them, favours the evolution of capitalism and, in the last resort, strengthens its staying power, delaying thereby the victory of socialism. Some of these radicals also see their enemy in international communism, maintaining that fear of it unites the capitalist countries overshadowing their divisive contradictions and conflicts and in this way constitutes an obstacle to the break up of the capitalist system.

In our country as well as among our emigrés, there are also some extreme radicals. They attempt to prove that detente and cooperation with the West only strengthens the Soviet bureaucracy, helping it to solve internal difficulties by means of foreign loans and commerce with the capitalist countries. This, they maintain, holds back the development of oppositional movements among the masses and is an obstacle to the breaking up of the hateful Soviet system of today. Of course, any deterioration in the economic situation of the West or of the East increases general dissatisfaction. And yet it is doubtful whether the situation in our respective countries would improve if the logic and influence of the extreme radicals were to prevail. In the West, as well as in the East, these people start from the premise: "The worse it is, the better." The anti-humanitarian character of this premise cannot be covered up by beautiful phrases and statements.

More difficult to discuss are the arguments of people who are in principle for detente, but criticise its present form and procedure. They find it does not go far enough, is equivocal, and insincere; and the price paid for it by the West is too high. They are against detente which has the character of a deal, or consists of various verbal assurances which can easily be disavowed. They warn that the USSR, regardless of detente, continues to increase its military potential and preserves its authoritarian system of government which makes it difficult to check whether agreements are really adhered to. They say that the Soviet Union has not repudiated its aims which are: class struggle and victory of Marxist socialism all over the world. Quite often they maintain that so far the Soviet Union has derived more benefit from detente than have the Western powers. They therefore demand that the West should agree to detente only if and when the Soviet Union grants considerable concessions in the field of democratization, and specifically, if it allows complete freedom of emigration as well as free movement of people, of ideas and information.

This tendency is reflected in the recent appeal of Academician A.D. Sakharov addressed to the new President and Congress of the USA. Sakharov calls for the acceptance of Senator Jackson's amendment in its previous "full" form, for rejection of all compromises and verbal promises, and for demanding not yearly emigration quotas, but general freedom to emigrate expressly guaranteed by law.

What can one say about such a viewpoint?

Academician Sakharov is basically correct, I think, when he points out that, in its present stage, detente is limited and too narrow, though some arguments of his co-thinkers raise reservations (for example of those who insist that detente benefits the USSR only). We too are of the opinion that Soviet citizens should be guaranteed freedom to emigrate and freedom to receive and spread ideas and information. However, we think it is not correct to tie all these various problems of detente and democratisation crudely into one knot and to demand that they should be solved at one go. The relaxation of tension is not a single act, but a protracted process, taking many years of which we are still at the very beginning. The imperfections of the internal structures of all the great powers are still so considerable that one cannot count on any speedy and radical changes. Obviously, every step on the road to detente should be achieved through concessions from both sides. But one should not yet expect concessions on a grand scale, and, quite especially, make demands which have the character of ultimatums. It is a very positive development that western societies begin not only to take an interest in the internal affairs of the USSR, but also to exercise pressure on our leaders in defence of democracy and humanitarianism. An excellent example of such a pressure was the protest of western intelligentsia against the forcible breaking up of the Moscow exhibition of abstract paintings. But it is unreasonable to put forward *at the very beginning* demands such as can be satisfied only as a *result* of the protracted process of detente. Conditions, which can be created only through progress and development, should not be put forward as preliminary terms.

True, in the negotiations between the great powers there are elements of scheming; but this is the result of weaknesses in the democratic structure not only of the USSR. Such deals about detente are still preferable to continued international tension or to secret deals about war.

In our world, so full of contradictions, there is no sensible alternative to the road towards gradual relaxation of tension. The people of the whole world are too tired of tension, of the arms race, of growing threat of war. Developed countries as well as the underdeveloped suffer in an equal degree, and today no government can brush these problems aside.

From what I have just said it is obvious that my disagreements with A.D. Sakharov concern certain questions of tactics only not the very fundamental principle of detente. Academician Sakharov is undoubtedly the most prominent fighter for the rights of man and his struggle, in the conditions of life in the USSR, also constitutes an important contribution to the cause of detente. This is why I fully agree with my brother Zhores, who at the Nobel Institute in Oslo declared that among people active today in the USSR, he saw nobody who would be a more worthy candidate for the Nobel Peace Prize than Academician Sakharov and that he would be glad if Sakharov were to receive the Prize for 1974.

It is very regrettable that some of my fellow-countrymen gave credence to the malicious falsification on this subject, falsifications which originated in the pages of an emigré journal deserving no confidence whatsoever. The fact that in the past Academician Sakharov took part in the construction of the most powerful section of Soviet armament obviously increases the importance and the weight of his present struggle for peace, for disarmament, and for the rights of man. After all, the founder of the Nobel Institute, Alfred Nobel, was himself the inventor of dynamite.

Today we are fully aware that peace and democracy on our planet depend not only on the intelligence and sense of responsibility of government leaders of great and small nations, but also on the action and initiative of all social forces and social movements.

September 1974

1. Prince Goremykin was the last but one Tsarist Prime Minister. *Translator's note.*
2. Nomenklatura — leading hierarchy, the Establishment — persons in high posts whose names appear on the Central Committee's register of important appointments. *Translator's note.*

4: Trade and Democratisation

The refusal of the Government of the USSR to implement the commercial agreement with the United States concluded in 1972 and recently ratified by the American Congress provoked consternation, as one could see from the comments of the foreign press, in certain political circles in Washington. The fact that the Government of the Soviet Union *on their own initiative* practically renounced the agreement towards which they had worked for a long time and for the sake of which they had already made a number of concessions in foreign and internal policy (concessions in truth, not too significant yet for all that unthinkable even four or five years earlier), is considered by many to be good reason to accuse the American Congress and even more so, Senator Jackson, of lack of foresight.

However, one cannot but realize that the unexpected decision of the Soviet government may have far-reaching consequences not only for the political future of Senator Jackson, but also for the whole process of detente between East and West, as well as for the economic development of the USSR. One should neither overestimate nor underestimate the importance of the many-sided and intensive commercial relations between the Soviet Union and the United States. The Soviet Union will no doubt incur a loss as a result of any decrease in trade with the USA, and the renunciation of the agreement was certainly, therefore, a difficult decision for the Soviet government. However, it is quite obvious to me that this decision was taken *unanimously*; it would be a mistake to ascribe it to the illness or diminished influence of any particular member of the Politbureau.

In spite of the fact that the Soviet press intentionally played down the decision, presenting it as an insignificant incident, it is, in reality, one of the most important events of the last decade. Moreover, it should not be considered from one side only, but should serve as an important lesson *for both sides*; according to the manner in which this lesson is learned, it may be the turning point on the road either to an improvement in the relations between the USSR and the USA, or their deterioration.

Far be it from me to treat the internal or foreign policy of the Soviet Union as beyond reproach, and quite particularly its policy on emigration. The American nation is made up mostly of immigrants who arrived from a dozen countries in the hope of finding a more secure life. Perhaps because of this, Americans have remained especially sensitive to the problems involving freedom of emigration, and in this matter exert an influence on their political leaders.

One should give due credit to the Secretary of State Kissinger, to Senator Jackson, and to American public opinion for having exercized such pressure as resulted in significant changes in Soviet emigration policy. But it would be a dangerous illusion to think that these concessions would become effective as rapidly and fundamentally as some people in the United States and in the USSR might wish. Ultimatums of any kind can only obstruct this process. Even more unacceptable to the Soviet leadership were various conditions incorporated by the American Congress into *American* legislation concerning emigration from the USSR.

If politics is the art of the possible, then Senator Jackson proved a bad politician, because he not only endeavoured to achieve the impossible, but also made quite an effort to present the difficult compromise, just arrived at, in a form humiliating for the USSR; moreover, for his own pretentious self-advertisement he used these concessions made by the Soviet Union, concessions which were the result of many protracted efforts of American public opinion as well as of the more sober part of the Soviet administration. Americans themselves can correctly ascertain the motives of their political leaders and decide how deeply Senator Jackson was really stirred by the tragic situation of the Soviet Jews and to what extent he used the tragedy of tens of thousands of Jewish families for the sake of his own personal career and in order to further some questionable political speculation.

Commercial relations are of exceptional importance to both countries. But certainly the question of trade should not have been so bluntly tied up with any specific quotas of Jewish emigration or with any setting up of deadlines and Commissions for "investigating" Soviet domestic policy. The adoption by Congress of a special law on trade left the Soviet government with no alternative but to take the decision they did.

If, however, the Soviet Government refused to submit to discriminatory clauses introduced by Congress because its prestige was at stake, then it must now refrain from unseemly pettiness, from placing ever renewed obstacles in the way of Jews or any other citizens who wish to emigrate. Moreover, it ought to do away with many existing obstacles and limitations. The point is not that such a step could facilitate a new round of negotiations on trade and detente, but that people, who for some reason are trying to leave the Soviet Union, should not be the subject of export deals. It is immoral to exchange individuals for roubles or dollars — as the authors of the ill-famed tax on education wished to do. But it is not less immoral to "buy" these individuals for dollar loans and technology, as Senator Jackson and his supporters sought to do.

Perhaps even more important was the question of American help in the investment of capital in Siberia. It is no secret that the Soviet leaders counted on credits, amounting to many millions, for the exploitation of very extensive oil and gas regions in the North and East of the USSR. The Americans have, however, decided to safeguard, in the immediate future (till 1985), their independent supply of energy. It was difficult to reconcile this decision with the granting of credits worth many millions for the exploration and exploitation of Siberian oil and gas. The repayment of credits and loans could only take the form of export of Siberian oil and gas to the USA; this would, of course, be contrary to the decision to limit or even to stop completely American import of foreign fuel.

The Soviet press has not been giving any prominence to this whole complex of contradictory economic schemes and expectations. It is understandable that every country is striving to safeguard its raw materials and fuel. But in most cases this problem defies solution. If we really wish to preserve peace and international cooperation, all such questions must be decided with due respect for the interests of all and on the basis of compromises commonly arrived at.

Various views concerning recent events have been current among Soviet dissidents. Those who have made up their minds solely in relation to their own emigration from the USSR, are a prey to real anxiety. There are others who maintain that the Soviet economy is in an impasse and that it cannot progress any further, and that a breach with the West would therefore contribute to the development of social consciousness and to bringing about a burst of spiritual energy among the Soviet people, too long trained in docility. I, for my part, should like to believe that these anxieties will prove groundless and that these dubious prophecies will remain unfulfilled.

January 1975

Part 2

The Discussion with Alexandr Solzhenitsyn

5: On Gulag Volume One

In this article I shall try to provide an evaluation of Solzhenitsyn's new book. The assessment can only be a brief and preliminary one – not merely because *Gulag Archipelago* is only the first of three or four volumes of a single work, but also because even by itself it is too considerable to be adequately appraised straightaway. The book is full of frightening facts: it would be difficult to grasp even a much smaller number of them immediately. Solzhenitsyn describes in concrete detail the tragic fate of hundreds of people, destinies both extraordinary and yet typical of what has befallen us in the past decades. His book contains many reflections and observations that are profound and truthful, and others which may not be correct, but are nevertheless always born from the monstrous sufferings of millions of people, in an agony unique in the age-old history of our nation. No man who left that terrible Archipelago was the same as he who entered it, either in body and health or in ideas about life and people. I believe that no-one who has read this book will remain the same person as he was when he opened its first pages. There is nothing in Russian or world literature in this respect which I can compare with Solzhenitsyn's work.

The Problem of Accuracy

A certain I. Soloviev has written in *Pravda* (14.1.74) that Solzhenitsyn's facts are unreliable fancies of a morbid imagination or mere cynical falsifications. This, of course, is not so. I cannot agree with some of Solzhenitsyn's judgements or conclusions. But it must be firmly stated that all the main facts in his book, and especially all the details of the life and torment of those who were imprisoned, from the time of their arrest to that of their death (or in rarer cases, their release) are perfectly correct. Of course, in an 'artistic investigation' on such a huge scale, based not only on the impressions of the author himself but also on stories told (and retold) by more than two hundred former prisoners, some inaccuracies are inevitable, particularly as Solzhenitsyn had to write his book in complete secrecy, with no possibility of discussing it before publication even with many of his close friends. But the number of these errors is very small in a work of such weight. My own calculation, for example, of the scale of the deportations from Leningrad after the murder of Kirov in 1934-5 is lower than that of Solzhenitsyn. Tens of thousands of people were deported, but not actually a quarter of the population of a city of 2,000,000. Yet I do not possess exact figures either, and base myself simply on fragmentary reports and my own impressions (I have lived in Leningrad for over 15 years). It is also difficult to believe the anonymous report that Ordzhonikidze could talk to old engineers with two revolvers on his desk, at his right and left hand. To seize former officials of the Tsarist régime (not, of course, all of them but mainly functionaries of the judiciary or gendarmerie), the GPU had no need to use random notes of casual informers. Lists of such officials could be found in local archives and in published reference books. In my view Solzhenitsyn exaggerates the number of peasants deported during the years of collectivization, which he estimates at 15 million. However, if one includes among the victims of those years peasants who died from starvation in 1932-3 (in the Ukraine alone not fewer than 3 to 4 million), it is possible to arrive at a figure even higher than that suggested by Solzhenitsyn. After Stalin's death, there were not ten but about a hundred officials of the MGB-MVD who were imprisoned or shot (in some cases without an open trial). But this was still a negligible number compared with the quantity of criminals from the "security organs" who were left at large or even given various responsible posts. In 1936-7 Bukharin was no longer a member of the Politbureau, as Solzhenitsyn claims, but was only a candidate-member of the Central Committee.

But all these and a few other inaccuracies are insignificant within the immense artistic investigation which Solzhenitsyn has undertaken. On the other hand, there are other "shortcomings" in the book which Solzhenitsyn himself notes in the dedication: he did not see everything, did not recollect everything, did not guess everything. He writes, for example, about the arrest of repatriated and amnestied Cossacks in the mid-1920s. But the campaign of mass terror against the Cossacks in the Don and Ural regions during the winter and spring of 1919 was still more terrible in its consequences. This campaign lasted "only" a little over two months, but it prolonged the Civil War with all its excesses for at least another year, providing the White Armies with dozens of new cavalry regiments. Then, too, there was the shooting of 500 hostages in Petrograd which the *Weekly Review* of the Cheka mentions in two lines . . . To describe it all many books are still needed; and I trust that they will be written.

If *Pravda* tried to argue that Solzhenitsyn's facts were untrue, *Literaturnaya Gazeta* by contrast (16.1.74) sought to persuade its readers that Solzhenitsyn's book contained nothing new. This is not true either. Although I have been studying Stalinism for over a decade, the book told me a great deal I had not known before. With the exception of former inmates of the camp, Soviet readers – even those who well remember the 20th and 22nd Congresses of the Party – know hardly one tenth of the facts recounted by Solzhenitsyn. Our youth, indeed, does not know even a one hundredth of them.

The Question of Vlassov

Many of our newspapers have written that Solzhenitsyn justifies, whitewashes, and even lauds Vlassov's Army. This is a deliberate and malignant distortion. Solzhenitsyn writes in *Gulag Archipelago* that the Vlassovites became pitiful hirelings of the Nazis, that they "were liable to trial for treason", that they took up the enemy's weapons and fought on the front with the despair of the doomed. Solzhenitsyn's own battery was nearly annihilated in East Prussia by Vlassovite fire. But Solzhenitsyn does not simplify the problem of Vlassov's troops and of similar formations in the fascist army.

Among the multiple waves of Stalinist repression, there were for many of us one that constituted our own special tragedy. For Tvardovsky, for instance, this was the destruction of the kulaks. His father, a poor and conscientious peasant, a former soldier in the Red Army, a defender of Soviet power, fell victim to it. He was deported to the Urals with his whole family. Only an accident saved his son: by that time he was already studying in an urban centre. This son was to become our great poet. But at that time Tvardovsky had to disown his father. He was to write about all this in his last poem *In the Name of Memory*.

For my own family, it was the repressions of 1937-8 that brought tragedy upon us, for the purges of those years struck especially at the commanders and commissars of the Red Army. My father, a divisional commander and lecturer at the Military Political Academy, was among those who were arrested and perished. Men like him were utterly devoted to the Soviet State, to the Bolshevik Party and to Socialism. They were romantic heroes to me as veterans of the Civil War, and I never believed that they were "enemies of the people".

For Solzhenitsyn, it was not his own arrest that was a profound personal tragedy, but the cruel and terrible fate of the millions of Soviet prisoners of war, his contemporaries, sons of October, who had in June 1941 formed a substantial part of the cadres of our army. This army was routed and surrounded in the first days and weeks of the war because of Stalin's criminal miscalculations, his inability to prepare the outbreak of hostilities, his desertion of his post in the first week of war, and his prior destruction of experienced commanders and commissars of whom there was now an acute shortage. About 3,000,000 soldiers and officers were taken prisoner in this debacle, and a further 1,000,000 subsequently captured in the "pincers" at Vyazma, Kharkov, on the Kerch Peninsula and near Volkhov. Stalin's régime then betrayed these soldiers a second time by refusing to sign the international prisoners-of-war convention, depriving them of all Red Cross aid and condemning them to starvation in German concentration camps. Finally, Stalin once again betrayed those who survived; after victory nearly all of them were arrested and sent to swell the population of Gulag Archipelago. Solzhenitsyn considers this terrible treason to its own troops to be the most odious single crime committed by the Stalinist régime — one unknown in the millenial annals of our nation. "I felt", writes Solzhenitsyn, "that the story of these millions of Russian prisoners would transfix me for ever, like a pin through a beetle."

Hardly one tenth of our prisoners joined Vlassov units, police sections, labour battalions, or "volunteered" for auxiliary brigades of the Wehrmacht. Most of those who did, genuinely hoped to acquire food and clothing, and then go over to the Soviet army or join the partisans. Such hopes soon proved illusory: the opportunities for crossing the lines were too small.

Solzhenitsyn does not justify and does not exalt these desperate and luckless men. But he pleads before the court of posterity the circumstances mitigating their responsibility. These youngsters were often not quite literate; the majority of them were peasants demoralized by the defeat; in captivity they were told that Stalin had disowned and vilified them; they found that this was true; and they knew that what awaited them was hunger and death in German camps.

Of course, it is not possible to assent to everything Solzhenitsyn says. For example, I feel no sympathy for a certain Yuri E. — a Soviet officer who consciously and without the compulsion of hunger went over to the Nazis and became a German officer in charge of an Intelligence training centre. From Solzhenitsyn's account, it is clear that this man returned to the Soviet Army only because of the complete rout of the Germans and not because he was drawn to his homeland; he banked on revealing "German secrets", in other words securing a transfer from the German Intelligence to the Soviet MGB. The same figure was apparently also convinced that a new war, between the USSR and the Allied would soon break out after the defeat of Germany, in which the Red Army would be swiftly defeated.

As for the violent battle which was fought near Prague between major Vlassovite units and German troops commanded by the SS General Steiner — this episode is an indisputable historical fact. Nearly all the "Vlassovites" were sentenced to 25 years' imprisonment. They never received any amnesty and virtually all of them perished in captivity and exile in the North. I share the view that this was too harsh a penalty for most of them. For Stalin was far more guilty than anyone else in this tragedy.

Solzhenitsyn has been accused of minimizing the evil of Nazism and the cruelty of Russian Tsarism. It was not Solzhenitsyn's task to provide an account of the "German Archipelago", although he frequently cites Gestapo tortures and the inhuman treatment of Russian prisoners of war by the fascists. But Solzhenitsyn does not depart from the truth, when he writes that Stalin unleashed mass repressions, deported millions of people, used torture and fabricated trials long before Hitler came to power. Moreover all this continued in our country many years after the defeat of German fascism.

Naturally, in this respect the Russian Tsars could hardly equal Stalin. Solzhenitsyn tells us a great deal about Tsarist prison and exile in his work, as this was a frequent topic of conversation among the prisoners, especially if there was an Old Bolshevik among them (prisoners belonging to the other socialist parties had nearly all died before the war). In such talks, prison and exile in the *ancien régime*

seemed like a rest-home to those who were in camps in the 1940s.
As for the scale of repression . . . In 1937-8, Stalin's apparatus shot
or starved to death in camps and prisons as many workers, peasants
and artisans in the course of a single day, as Tsarist executioners
killed in a year at the time of the 1905 revolution and the reaction
which followed it. There is simply no comparison.

I suspect that different readers will find that different chapters of
Solzhenitsyn's book make the most powerful impression on them.
For me the most important were "Blue Edgings" (Chapter Four) and
"The Supreme Penalty" (Chapter Eleven). In these the author
achieves an exceptional depth of psychological insight into the behaviour of prison guards and their victims. Solzhenitsyn is profound-
er here than Dostoyevsky. I do not mean by this that Solzhenitsyn
is a greater artist than Dostoyevsky. I am not a specialist on literature. But it is clear that the Stalinist prisons, camps, transit centres
and exiles that Solzhenitsyn traversed a hundred years after the
arrest and exile of Dostoyevsky, gave him ten times as many opportunities to study the various forms of human evil as the author
of *The House of the Dead* had. There is no doubt that Solzhenitsyn
has acquitted himself of this task as only a great writer would.

Gulag Archipelago contains many penetrating and accurate, although incidental, remarks about Stalin's personality. Solzhenitsyn
considers, however, that Stalin's personal role in the historical catastrophe which struck our country, and even in the creation of the
Archipelago, was so unimportant that many of these remarks are
dropped outside the main text, relegated to parentheses and foot-
notes. Thus in the footnote on the penultimate page of the book, we
read: "Both before and during my time in prison, I too used to believe that Stalin was responsible for the disastrous course taken by
the Soviet State. Then Stalin died peacefully – and has the direction
of the ship changed in the least? His own personal imprint on events
was merely a dreary stupidity, an obtuse vanity. For the rest, he
simply followed where footsteps made before him led."

Solzhenitsyn treats only very briefly, in his second chapter, the
repressions of 1937-8 (why give details of 'what has already been
widely described and will frequently be repeated again'?) when the
core of the party leadership, intelligentsia, officers and commissars
of the Red Army, and the majority of prominent economic adminis-
trators and Komsomol leaders, were liquidated in the cellars of the

On Gulag Volume One

67

NKVD, and when the stop State leadership together with the senior ranks of the security apparatus, the diplomatic service, and so on, were violently reshuffled. Solzhenitsyn comments, again in a footnote: 'Today the evidence of the Cultural Revolution in China (also 17 years after final victory), suggests in all probability the operation here of a general law of history. Even Stalin himself now begins to seem a mere blind and superficial instrument of it.'

It is difficult to agree with such a view of Stalin's role and importance in the tragedy of the thirties. It would, of course, be a mistake to separate the epoch of Stalinist terror completely from the revolutionary period that preceded it. There was no such precise or absolute boundary line either in 1937 as many believe, or in 1934 as Khrushchev maintained, or in 1929 as Solzhenitsyn himself once thought, or in 1924, when Lenin died and the Trotskyist Opposition was broken up, or in 1922 when Stalin became the General Secretary of the Party. Yet all these years, and also others, marked political turning points that were extremely real and demand special analysis.

Obviously there exists a continuity between the party which took power in October 1917 and that which governed the USSR in 1937, in 1947, in 1957, and in 1967 when Solzhenitsyn was completing *Gulag Archipelago*. But this continuity is not synonymous with identity. Stalin did not always follow in "footsteps made before him". In the first years of the revolution he certainly did not always follow in Lenin's footsteps; in fact, even then, with every step he led the party in another direction. Outer similarities marked very great inner divergences, and in some cases even polar opposites; and the road to these was in no way pre-determined by an inevitable law of history. A deeper and more scientific analysis of the events discussed by Solzhenitsyn in his artistic investigation, will in the future incontrovertibly show that even within the framework of the relations between Party, State, and society created in Russia under Lenin, Stalin effected sharp turns and fundamental reversals, merely preserving the outward shell of so-called Leninist norms and the official vocabulary of Marxism-Leninism. Stalinism was in many respects the negation and bloody annihilation of Bolshevism and of all revolutionary forces in Russia: it was in a determinate sense a genuine counter-revolution. Of course, this does not mean that the Leninist period and heritage in the history of the Russian Revolution should be exempted from the most serious critical analysis.

It was not Solzhenitsyn's purpose to study the phenomenon of Stalinism — its nature and specificity, its evolution and presuppositions. For Solzhenitsyn, the very concept of Stalinism is apparently non-existent, since Stalin merely "followed where footsteps made before him led". In his book there is nothing which one might call an historical background.

The work begins with the chapter entitled 'Arrest' — a device wherewith the author stresses at the outset that he will investigate and describe only the world of the prisoners, the realm of the rejected, the secret and terrible region of the archipelago, its geography, its structure, its social relations, its written and unwritten laws, its population, its manners, its customs, its potentates and subjects. In fact, Solzhenitsyn has no need of an historical background, for his Archipelago appears on the map already in 1918 and thereafter develops according to a kind of internal law of its own. This one-sidedness, occasionally offset by a few very profound remarks, dominates the whole volume. Solzhenitsyn is, of course, perfectly entitled to treat his subject in this way.

Paradoxically, however, without ever really speaking of Stalinism and even purporting to deny its legitimacy as a concept, Solzhenitsyn's artistic investigation of one of the main sectors of the Stalinist régime, helps us to comprehend the whole criminal inhumanity of Stalinism as a system. Solzhenitsyn is not correct when he contends that this system has essentially survived to this day; but neither has it disappeared completely from our social, political, and cultural life. Solzhenitsyn has dealt a very heavy blow to Stalinism and neo-Stalinism with this book. None of us has done more in this respect than Solzhenitsyn.

Solzhenitsyn and Lenin

Even when he was a Komsomol, Solzhenitsyn had his doubts about the wisdom and honesty of Stalin. It was precisely these misgivings, expressed in one of his letters from the front, that led to his arrest and conviction. But at that time he still never doubted that "the great October Revolution was splendid and just, a victorious accomplishment of men animated by high purpose and self-sacrifice". Today, Solzhenitsyn thinks otherwise, both about the October Revolution and about Lenin.

Here we shall deal with only two accusations, from among the great number that Solzhenitsyn now levels directly or indirectly against Lenin. Solzhenitsyn contends that in 1917 Lenin was determined to force Russia through a new "proletarian and social-ist" revolution, although neither Russia nor the Russian people needed such a revolution, or were ready for it. He also maintains that Lenin misused terrorist methods of struggle against his political opponents. It is, of course, easy to point to mistakes made by a revolutionary 50 years after the event. But the first socialist revolu-tion was inevitably a leap into the unknown. There was no precedent for it, no comparative experience from which its leaders could benefit. It was impossible to weigh up every eventuality beforehand, and only then take careful decisions. Events could be predicted at most for days or weeks ahead. Fundamental decisions were made, and methods of revolutionary struggle adopted or corrected, only in the vortex of events themselves. Lenin was well aware of this, and often repeated Napoleon's maxim: *On s'engage et puis on voit.* No revolution can be made without taking risks – risks of defeat, and risks of error. But a revolutionary party is also risking a great deal if it does not give the signal for revolution, when a revolution is possible. It is not surprising that Lenin and his government commit-ted a series of mistakes and miscalculations. The mistakes prolonged and exacerbated the Civil War. The miscalculations initially increased the economic disarray in the country, and delayed the transition to NEP. Lenin's hopes of an imminent European revolution that would come to the technical and cultural aid of Russia did not materialize. The Soviet government went too far in restricting democracy in our country.

The list of such errors and miscalculations could be extended. But no cybernetics will ever be able to prove that the armed uprising of 24 October 1917 was historically a premature action, and that all the future misdeeds of Stalin's regime followed from this fatal mistake by Lenin. For after Lenin's death the party still had to choose paths explored by no predecessor. Unfortunately, those who succeeded Lenin at the head of the party did not possess his wisdom, his knowledge, or his ability usually to find the right solutions for difficult situations. They did not make even minimal use of the op-portunities which the October Revolution had created for a rapid advance towards a genuinely socialist and democratic society. Today we still remain far from that objective. Stalin not only did not "follow exactly where footsteps made before him led". Such "footsteps" do not exist in history. In fact, Stalin swiftly rejected the few guidelines left by Lenin in his last writings.

In conditions of Revolution and Civil War, no government can dispense with forms of violence. But even the most objective historian would have to say that already in the first years of Soviet power the reasonable limits of such violence were frequently overstepped. From the summer of 1918, a wave of both White and Red terror broke over our country. A great many of these acts of mass violence were quite unnecessary and harmful to the logic and interest of the class struggle itself. Such terror merely brutalised both sides, prolonged the war and generated further superfluous violence. It is unfortunately true that in the early years of the Revolution, Lenin too used the verb "shoot" much more often than existing circumstances demanded. Solzhenitsyn cites Lenin, without actually distorting his words, but always with a disobliging comment. Nevertheless, would anyone today approve, for example, of the following order sent in August 1918 by Lenin to G. Fedorov, head of the local Soviet in the province of Nizhni Novgorod: "No efforts to be spared; mass terror to be introduced, *hundreds* of prostitutes who have intoxicated our soldiers, and former officers, etc, to be shot and deported."[1] Deport — yes, but why kill women?

Such abuses of power must be regretted and condemned. Yet the terror of the Civil War did not pre-determine the fearful terror of the Stalinist epoch. Lenin made not a few mistakes, many of which he admitted himself. There is no doubt that an honest historian must take note of his errors and abuses of power. However, we remain convinced that the overall balance sheet of Lenin's activity was positive. Solzhenitsyn thinks otherwise. That is his right. In a socialist country, every citizen should be able to express his opinions and judgements on the activity of any political leader.

The Example of Krylenko

In his book Solzhenitsyn does not spare any of the revolutionary parties in Russia. The SR's (Socialist-Revolutionaries) were terrorists and babblers, "with no worthy leaders". The Mensheviks were naturally only babblers. But it is the Bolsheviks whom Solzhenitsyn condemns most fiercely: although they were able to seize and hold power in Russia, in doing so they gave proof of excessive and needless cruelty. Among the Bolshevik leaders, Solzhenitsyn singles out in particular N.V. Krylenko, the Chairman of the Supreme Revolutionary Tribunal and Procurator of the Republic, the chief prosecutor in the "show" trials of the first years of the Soviet regime. Solzhenitsyn devotes nearly two whole chapters to these trials ("The Law – a Child", "The Law Matures"). Krylenko's name also makes a frequent appearance in other chapters.

Of course, it can be pointed out that the first years of Soviet power were the time of the most desperate struggle of the Soviet Republic for its very survival. If Revolution and Soviet power were necessary, then they had to be defended against numerous and merciless foes; and this could not have been accomplished without revolutionary-military tribunals and the Cheka. But even bearing all this in mind, it is impossible to shut one's eyes to the fact that many of the sentences meted out in "court" and out of court were unjust or senselessly brutal, and that many extraneous, stupid and malevolent elements were given in the Cheka and in the tribunals. Krylenko soon became one of the main "directors" of this repression, playing a role similar to that of the Jacobin tribune Couthon, who sent to the guillotine not only Royalists, but also simple old women of 70 and young girls of 18, revolutionaries discontented with Robespierre, and the eminent chemist Lavoisier (who requested time to complete an important series of experiments before his execution – "We do not need scientists," replied Couthon).

Of course, Krylenko was not an isolated exception within the ranks of the Bolsheviks. But neither were all the leaders of that party like him. Unfortunately, however, it is not only the most honest and courageous men of their time who become revolutionaries. A revolution, especially during its ascent, also attracts people who are resentful, vain, ambitious, self-seeking, men of cold hearts and unclean hands, as well as many stupid and obtuse fanatics capable of anything. But all this is no reason to condemn every revolution and every revolutionary.

Something else has also to be considered. For the Russian revolutionaries, their greatest test proved to be neither imprisonment nor exile in Siberia, neither reckless attack under fire from White Guards' machine-guns, nor hunger and cold, but *power* and especially the practically unlimited power of the first phase of the Soviet regime. It has long been known that power corrupts and depraves even some of the best of men. It must be admitted with sadness that very many Bolsheviks did not withstand the ordeal of power. Long before their own destruction in the grinding machine of Stalinist persecutions, the same people participated in many acts of cruel repression against others, which in most cases were unjust, gratuitous and harmful. But it in no way follows from this that these Bolsheviks were equally unjust or cruel, or insensitive to human suffering, before the Revolution — indeed that they had not been inspired by the best of motives and by the highest of aims and ideals.

Solzhenitsyn understands the corrupting influence of power. He describes with utter candour how, after a hard and hungry year as an ordinary private, deadened by drill and discipline, bullied by stripling officers, he forgot all this completely the moment he himself became a lieutenant and then a captain. He started to develop a deep mental gulf between himself and his subordinates; he understood less and less the heavy burdens of existence on the front; he saw himself more and more as a man of a different kind and caste. Without giving it a second thought, he availed himself of all the privileges accorded to officers, arrogantly addressed old and young alike, harassed his orderly, and was sometimes so harsh to his men that on one occasion an old colonel had to rebuke him during an inspection. Solzhenitsyn confesses: "From the officer's epaulettes that decorated by shoulders for a mere two years, a poisonous golden dust filtered into the void between my ribs." Moreover, Solzhenitsyn nearly became an officer in the NKVD itself: attempts were made to persuade him to enter the NKVD school and had further pressure been applied, he would have consented. Recalling his career as an officer, he makes the merciless admission: "I thought of myself as a selfless and disinterested person. Yet I had meanwhile become a ready-made hangman. Had I gone to school in the NKVD under Yezhov, I would have been fully-fledged under Beria."

If Solzhenitsyn changed so much during his two years as a junior officer, then what is likely to have happened to Krylenko — who in an even shorter period of time rose, so to speak, from ensign to supreme command in the Russian army and then became President of the Supreme Revolutionary Tribunal, Deputy Commissar for Justice and Chief Procurator of the RSFSR? Although Krylenko had finished two academic courses before the Revolution, so much accumulated power made him drunk and stupid beyond all recognition.

"It seems", Solzhenitsyn writes, "that evil has its own threshold of magnitude too. A man may balance and toss between good and evil all his life, slip down, let go, lift himself up again, repent, then fall into darkness once more – but as long as he has not crossed a critical threshold of evil, he may yet redeem himself, there is still hope for him. But when the baseness of his misdeeds or the absoluteness of his power reaches a certain point, he suddenly crosses that threshold, and then he abandons humanity. Perhaps then – there is no return."

"Let the reader who expects to find a political indictment here, close this book," writes Solzhenitsyn elsewhere. "Oh, if everything were so simple! – if somewhere there were dark men cunningly plotting dark deeds, and it were enough to uncover and destroy them. But the line that divides good from evil runs through every man's heart; and who would destroy part of his own heart? . . . In the lifetime of one heart this line is always moving, now compressed by triumphant evil, now yielding space to awakening goodness. The very same man at different ages, in different situations of his life is often a wholly different person. At one moment, he may be near diabolic; at another near saintly. But his name does not change, and we attribute all his actions alike to it." In this profound remark, we can perceive at least part of the explanation for the drama and fall of very many Bolsheviks, who were by no means the smallest of cogs in the early machinery of arbitrary rule, before they themselves became victims of Stalinist terror.

Solzhenitsyn's Own Proposals

But if power corrupts and depraves men, if politics is, as Solzhenitsyn believes, "not even a form of science – but an empirical field, which cannot be defined by mathematical formula, subject to human egoism and blind passion", if all professional politicians are no more than "carbuncles on the neck of society preventing the free movement of its head and arms", then what should we strive for, how can we build a just human community?

Solzhenitsyn deals with these questions only incidentally, in parenthetic remarks, which are not explained or developed in detail. But is is clear from these brief comments that Solzhenitsyn considers the justest form of society to be one "headed by people who are capable of rationally directing its activities". For Solzhenitsyn, such people are in the first instance technicians and scientists (workers, in Solzhenitsyn's view, only as assistants to technicians in industry). But who would assume the moral leadership of such a society? His reflections make it clear that for him it is not a political doctrine, but only religion that can fulfil this moral function. Belief in God is the sole moral bulwark of humanity, and deeply religious people alone bore well — better than all others — the sufferings of Stalin's camps and prisons.

But such thoughts are a surrender to Utopia, and they are not even very original. Solzhenitsyn hits out violently against every sort of political falsehood. He rightly calls on Soviet people, and above all on Soviet youth, not to assist or collude with lies. But it is not enough only to convince people of the falsity of this or that political doctrine; it is also necessary to show them the truth elsewhere and to convince them of its real value. However, for the overwhelming majority of the Soviet population, religion does not and cannot any longer represent such a truth. The youth of this century are scarcely likely to be guided by faith in God. Indeed, without politics and political struggle, how could engineers and scientists ever undertake to direct the affairs of a society or its economy? Moreover, even if they succeeded, what would prevent such a society from becoming a dictatorship of technocrats? If religion were to gain moral dominance of society once more, would this not eventually reproduce the worst forms of theocracy?

Referring to the repressions of 1937, Solzhenitsyn writes: "Perhaps 1937 was *necessary,* to prove how worthless was the *world outlook* which they vaunted, while they tore Russia asunder, destroying her bulwarks and trampling her shrines." Solzhenitsyn's allusion, as may readily be guessed, is to Marxism. But here he is mistaken. It was not Marxism that was responsible for the perversions of Stalinism, and the supersession of Stalinism will in no way mean the collapse of Marxism or of scientific socialism. Solzhenitsyn is well aware of the fact, which he mentions on another page, that the two-hundred-year-old savagery of the Inquisition, with its burning and torturing of heretics, was eventually mitigated by, among other things, religious ideology itself.

To me, at any rate, Solzhenitsyn's ideals have very little appeal. I remain deeply convinced that in the foreseeable future our society will have to be based on the unity of socialism and democracy, and that it is precisely the development of Marxism and scientific communism that alone can permit the creation of a just human community.

Technicians and researchers should have a greater say in our society than they enjoy today. But this in no way precludes a scientifically organised political system. Such a system would involve, in particular, abolition of all privileges for public leaders, a rational limitation of political power, self-administration wherever possible, increased jurisdiction for local authorities, separation of legislative, executive and judicial powers, restriction of incumbency of political positions to limited periods of time, full freedom of thought and expression (including, of course, religious conviction and practice), liberty of organisation and assembly for representatives of all political currents, free elections and equal rights to put forward candidates for all political groups and parties, and so on. Only such a society, free from the exploitation of man by man and based on common ownership of the means of production, can ensure an unimpeded and comprehensive progress of all mankind, as well as of every individual.

So long as we have not achieved full socialist democracy in the USSR, the development of our country will continue to remain slow, partial and deformed, and spiritual giants like Solzhenitsyn will be rare. Before his arrest, Solzhenitsyn considered himself a Marxist. After the terrible experiences described with such implacable truth in *Gulag Archipelago,* Solzhenitsyn lost belief in Marxism. This is a matter of his conscience and his conviction. Every sincere change of belief deserves respect and understanding. Solzhenitsyn did not deceive or betray anybody. Today he is an opponent of Marxism, and does not hide the fact.

Marxism will not, of course, collapse through the loss of one of its former adherents. We believe, on the contrary, Marxism can only benefit from polemical debate with an opponent like Solzhenitsyn. It is obviously far better for Marxism to have adversaries like Solzhenitsyn than "defenders" like Mikhalkov or Chakovsky.[2] A "scientific" ideology which has to be imposed on people by sheer force or the threat of force is worthless. Fortunately, genuine scientific socialism has no need of such methods.

1. Lenin, *Collected Works,* (Russian edition). Vol.50, p.142.
2. Sergei Mikhalkov and Alexander Chakovsky: leading functionaries of the Soviet Writers' Union.

6: On Gulag Volume Two

General Evaluation

The second volume of Solzhenitsyn's *The Gulag Archipelago* has now appeared in print. While the first described in detail all that went on before millions of Soviet citizens found themselves in Stalinist concentration camps: the system of arrests and various aspects of confinement to prisons, the process of interrogation and investigation, judicial and non-judicial tribunals; deportations and transit camps; in the second volume the author examines the main and essential part of the Gulag Empire – the "corrective", or as he rightly calls them "destructive-labour camps". Nothing escapes his attention: the origins and history of the camps, the economics of forced labour, the administrative set up, various categories of prisoners and their everyday existence, the situation of women and children, the relationship between ordinary inmates and the "trusties", between the criminal and political prisoners, questions of security, of convoys, of information, of the recruitment of stool-pigeons, the system of punishment and "incentives", the role of hospitals and medical centres, different ways of dying, different forms of assassination, and the uncomplicated ceremony of burials – all this finds its expression in Solzhenitsyn's book. He describes various aspects of hard labour, the convicts' starvation régime; he reveals not only the world of the camps, but also that adjacent to it, one of the "free workers" – "The Campside", as well as the peculiar psychological problem of the relations between the convicts and their jailers.

Like the first volume, published in December 1973, the second deserves the highest praise, especially because Solzhenitsyn's scrupulous artistic investigation is based on authentic facts. True, the second volume does not have the same shocking, mortifying, and sickening effect as the first, perhaps because it is the second. Or possibly this impression is due to the fact that I had already read a great many memoirs of former inmates (most of which, of course, have never been published), and jotted down hundreds of stories and eye-witness accounts of camp life. It is also significant that, together with the authentic t sic facts (there are noticeably fewer inaccuracies in this volume than in the previous one), the author offers many opinions and judgements which are too one-sided and categorical; moreover, his generalizations are not always necessarily well founded. This happens especially when in painting the "free world" he uses highly condensed hues.

All the shortcomings mentioned here do not detract, of course, from the artistic and social importance of the book which has no equal in the whole of our "Gulag" literature.

One of the former "sons of the Gulag" who visited Vorkuta as a free man (many, as Solzhenitsyn says, are tempted to see again those places where for years they had worked behind barbed wires) related to me quite a common occurrence: on an abandoned camp site building work was started as foundations had to be laid for a new school. When the excavator removed the first thin layer of soil, an enormous heap of human bones was uncovered. It was not, of course, a pre-historic site and no archaeologists ever came to inspect it. This was one of the huge common graves of the northern camps, one of those pits dug up in the autumn into which during the whole winter thousands of corpses of those who died or had been shot were thrown to be covered with earth during the short northern summer. The building of the school was for a time interrupted, but not in order to raise a monument to the memory of unknown prisoners. During the night the bones were transported and buried somewhere beyond the boundary of the town, and this new cemetery was not in any way marked either. A school was finally built on the site of the previous fraternal grave. We have little hope that even where the biggest camps were, memorials will be raised, that museums with barracks, zones, watch-towers, will be put up so that some *in memoriam* will mark the innumerable cemeteries where probably more Soviet people lie buried than have perished in the years of the Great Patriotic War. There is little hope that here an eternal flame will burn and the names of the dead and the killed will be engraved on marble slabs. Maybe only books will remain as monuments to their memory. *The Gulag Archipelago*, dedicated to those who perished in the camps and who, in the words of the author "had not lived to tell the story", will outlive its persecutors and will never be forgotten.

The myths

In our country, where no freedom of the press and information exists, where most news is spread through some concealed channels, inevitably there circulate a great number of rumours and dozens of various legends which by many are taken as absolute truth. Even more so in the conditions of camp life all kinds of legends, rumours, and myths must have been conceived that were often very far from the truth. Natalya Reshetovskaya tried recently to prove that Solzhenitsyn's book is also essentially built on such concentration camp folklore. This is, of course, not correct. It was not Solzhenitsyn's fault that he could not verify many of the accounts which he heard from his co-prisoners and informants. However, his own camp experience as well as his artistic intuition allowed him in written reports to separate, convincingly, the truth from surmises in the majority of instances. If, in rare cases, some legend finds its way onto the pages of the book, this happens mainly when he deals with the distant past or with the life and "business" of people at the top of the administrative machinery (e.g. with Abakumov, the Minister of State Security).

I think that as one of such legends is the story of the 14-year old boy, who on 20 June 1929, during the visit of Maxim Gorky to the Solovetsky camp asked to remain with him alone and related to the famous writer, during an hour and a half, all the iniquities perpetrated there. According to Solzhenitsyn, Gorky after the talk with the boy, came out of the room with tears in his eyes. Yet not only did he do nothing for the inmates of Solovky, but many times praised the Solovky Chekists while the same night the truth-loving boy was shot by the same Chekists. On the other hand, Solzhenitsyn himself says that it was only in the middle of March 1929 that the first batch of youngsters arrived at Solovky. How then could a boy, isolated from adults in a children's colony, and new to the camp, know all that had been going on for years there? However, even if this incident seems dubious, Solzhenitsyn's own story, supported by other reports, about the lawlessness and the many horrors in the camp, does not raise any doubt.

How the camps came into being

According to Solzhenitsyn, the establishment of concentration camps for political enemies dates from the year 1918. This is not a

slander as some of his opponents maintain. Solzhenitsyn quotes a
telegram from Lenin to the head of the Penza Executive Committee,
Yevgenia Bosch, in which Lenin advised her "to lock up all suspects
in a concentration camp outside the city". (Lenin, *Collective Works,*
5th Russian ed. v.50, p.143-44). One could also adduce other official
documents to this effect. In the text of a special decision taken by
the Council of People's Commissars of the RSFSR of 5 September
1918, we read: ". . . It is necessary to protect the Soviet Republic
from class enemies by isolating them in concentration camps"
(*Cheka Weekly Review* no.1, 22 September 1918, p.II.) In February
1919, G. Sokolnikov, member of the Central Committee of the
Revolutionary War Committee and the War Soviet of the Southern
Front, objected to the Central Committee's directive concerning the
"anti-Cossack campaign" (the mass shooting of Cossacks who were
helping General Krasnov or serving in his White Army). Sokolnikov
proposed not to execute them but to make them do useful work in
coal mining, road building, slate and peat production. For this purpose Sokolnikov demanded by cable that "the establishment of
labour camps be immediately undertaken". (Central Party Archives.)
At the time of the civil war concentration camps were quite primitive
and their régime bore very little resemblance to that of the 1930s.
Sometimes prisoners were set to work. In other cases, when near the
frontline districts a site outside the town was enclosed, the imprisoned "socially dangerous elements" did no work. Food was
brought to them by family and friends and handed across the fence.
It is clear from the Cheka documents that at the end of 1920 the
majority of inmates consisted of peasants arrested for "speculation".
With the conclusion of the civil war many of these camps were
liquidated and the prisoners sent home. With the beginning of NEP
the camps for political prisoners were apparently completely dis-
mantled (apart from the Solovetsky Island Special camp and some
"Isolators" about which Solzhenitsyn writes).

We cannot discuss here the question of how much in those distant
days the existence of the camps was dictated by the harsh necessities
of the time or how much was simply a useless and uncalled for arbitrariness. But it would be a mistake to make no distinction between
the camps in the period of the civil war and those of the Stalin era,
or to ignore the fact that in 1918-1920 the Soviet Republic was
engaged in a war simultaneously against several white régimes

supported by interventionist forces, and that in many concentration camps, established on the territories in the hands of the Whites and the interventionist armies, the oppression was, more often than not, even worse than in the camps within the RSFSR. In Stalin's time the terror of concentration camps was directed against helpless, unarmed people, who were not dangerous to the strong and unified authority firmly established in the country. For Solzhenitsyn this difference does not seem to exist.

The flood of 1937

Solzhenitsyn does not conceal his hostility towards those party and state officials, those high commanders of the Red Army, those leading cadres of the Comsomol and the Trade Unions organisation, and especially towards the leading functionaries of the NKVD and the Office of Public Prosecutor who themselves became the victims of cruel persecution in 1937 and 1938. Already in the first volume of *The Gulag Archipelago* Solzhenitsyn wrote: "If you study in detail the whole history of the arrests and trials of 1936 to 1938, the principal revulsion you feel is not against Stalin and his accomplices but against the humiliatingly repulsive defendants — nausea at their spiritual baseness after their former pride and implacability." All these people, according to Solzhenitsyn, had been pitiless vis-à-vis their political opponents during the years of the civil war or collectivisation and industrialisation and therefore did not merit any sympathy when "the system" turned against them.

We find the same attitude towards "the flood of 1937" on the pages of the second volume too. With obvious satisfaction the author lists the names of tens of prominent leaders of the Communist party shot on Stalin's orders in 1937-38. They got what they deserved, they got what they did to others:

> "And though, when the young Tukhachevsky returned victorious from suppressing the devastated Tambov peasants, there was no Marya Spiridonova waiting at the station to put a bullet through his head, it was done 16 years later by the Georgian priest who never graduated."

We cannot possibly share such views and attitudes. First of all, one should not ignore that among the victims of the 1930s there were leaders who greatly differed from each other, not only in their personal qualities, but also in the degree to which they were responsible for the lawlessness of the preceding years. There were, among them, people already deeply depraved, already in the grip of the Stalinist system to such an extent that without a thought they were ready to execute the most cruel and inhuman orders, caring neither for their country, nor for its people, but only for themselves and their power. Such men not only executed orders, but even "showed initiative", helped Stalin and the NKVD in "unmasking" and destroying "the enemies of the people". But there were also not a few who were misguided, who were at the same time the weapon and the victim of another cult — of the cult of party discipline. There were among them many honest, devoted and brave men who came to understand much when it was already too late. There were not a few despairing at what was happening in the country and yet believing the party and its propaganda. Maybe one can talk today about the historico-political guilt of the whole body of party activists for the events of the 1920s and 1930s. But in no way can one treat all these people wholesalely as criminals who got what they deserved. The fate of the majority of revolutionary Bolsheviks remains one of the most terrible tragedies in the history of our country and we cannot support Solzhenitsyn who sneeringly proposes to change, in the obituaries of these people, the words "tragically perished at the time of the cult of personality" into "comically perished . . .". The best Russian writers never allowed themselves to mock the dead. Let us recall Pushkin's words: "It is true that Ryazgo against Ferdinand sinned. For this he was hanged. Would it be dignified on our part to jeer at the victim of the hangman?"

When I read the first volume of *The Archipelago*, I was disagreeably struck by Solzhenitsyn's admission that the thought of humiliations inflicted in the Butyrki prison on N. Krylenko, the former Minister of Justice, before he was shot, the same Krylenko who himself had humiliated others — somehow "reassured" him when he was describing the trials at which Krylenko took part as a prosecutor. It seems that such an attitude is very far from the simple humanity, from the "undogmatic judgement", not to mention the Christian principles of "charity and understanding" about which Solzhenitsyn preaches at the end of the book.

This attitude of Solzhenitsyn seems to us erroneous not only because, as it is well-known, the exterminated Soviet and party leaders were replaced more often than not by men who proved worse: at the time of Yezhov and Beria one regretted the departure of Chekists like Latsis and Peters. Their harshness, justified or not, was never dictated by self-seeking, by servility or sadism; they could not, probably, have gone as far on the road of criminality as Yezhov, Beria, Zakovsky, and their like did.

One should clearly state that no man deserved the terrible fate that befell the leaders arrested in 1937-38. And it is impossible to relish the thought of their humiliations and sufferings, even if one does know that many of them deserved the penalty of death.

In one of his stories from Kolyma V. Shalamov tells about the tragedy of Nikonov, the deputy commander of the Ukrainian NKVD and one of Yezhov's and Zakovsky's collaborator, whose testicles were crushed during "interrogation" (about this method of torture, the most unbearable one, Solzhenitsyn wrote in his first volume). Reading Shalamov I did not experience any feeling of satisfaction. It is quite possible that this Nikonov fully deserved to be condemned to death and shot for his crimes. Morally, it is wrong to think that Stalin's warfare against the main cadres of the party and State, even in its most perverse form, resulted in some triumph of historic justice. Not at all. The destruction of these men became a prologue to the triumph of even more terrible injustices — not only towards the party but towards our whole country.

In a strange way Solzhenitsyn seems ready to admit that the whole Soviet nation, that all Russian and non-Russian citizens deserved the grievous fate that befell them between the 1920s and 1940s. Already in the first volume he exclaimed having in mind not so much the party as the most ordinary people: "We spent ourselves in one unrestrained outburst in 1917, and then we *hurried* to submit. We submitted with *pleasure* . . . We purely and simply *deserved* everything that happened afterwards." (Vol.I, p.13, Solzhenitsyn's italics). There are quite a few similar statements also in·the second volume of *The Archipelago.* The incorrectness and injustice of such a judgement seems so obvious that it would be a waste of time to refute it further.

Communist prisoners of the Gulag

It seems that the majority of those shot in 1937-1938 were communists. However, hundreds of thousands of rank and file communists and Comsomol middle cadres were also, together with other prisoners, dispatched to concentration camps. To these communists Solzhenitsyn devotes one of his chapters, though he writes a great deal about them in other parts of the book too. He deals briefly with those "for whom [their] Communist faith was an inner thing" and was "not constantly on the tips of their tongues", who were neither parading their "partyness" nor "incessantly declaiming about it" and distancing themselves from other prisoners. He gives his main attention to the "orthodox" ones and to the "Loyalists" — the chapter bears this title. These "loyalists" tried to exonerate Stalin; marching in convoys they sang "I know no other country when man breathes so freely"; they considered nearly all other prisoners justly condemned, but saw themselves as victims of a misunderstanding. Solzhenitsyn finds many reasons to make fun of such "loyalist" and "orthodox" types. Sometimes they fully deserve his irony. It is true that quite a number of communists arrested in 1937-38 continued to believe not only in Stalin but also in Yezhov; they kept themselves apart from their fellow-prisoners and were even hostile to them. But very soon they regained their sight, though perhaps not always fully: after some months of "interrogation" the number of "loyalists" and "orthodox" party men would dwindle. There were not many such people in the camps anyhow; but for the majority of communists the condemnation of Stalin and of the NKVD was not by any means equivalent to the renunciation of their socialist and communist convictions.

Clearly, Solzhenitsyn is guilty of misrepresentation when he states that the communists in the camps "did not object to the dominance of the thieves in the kitchens and among the trusties" and that "All the orthodox Communists [were] soon going to get themselves well fixed up". He even puts forward the following hypothesis: ". . . were there not perhaps some written or at least oral directives: to make things easier for the Communists?".

No, Alexander Solzhenitsyn, there was never any such directive, and you knew this perfectly well when in your *One Day in the Life of Ivan Denisovich* you related how the Communist Buynovsky was thrown into a freezing punishment cell without any justification whatsoever. No. On the basis of the experiences of Boris Dyakov and Galina Serebryakov one cannot draw general conclusions about the situation and behaviour of the bulk of the imprisoned communists. In many respects their lot was even worse than that of other categories of prisoners, and not fewer but perhaps more of them found their death in Stalinist camps. Of course, about all this there are no reliable statistics. However, from documents of party conferences which took place after the XXII Congress of the CPSU we do know that in 1955-57 about 6 per cent of party members arrested in 1936-38 returned to Moscow. The remaining 94 per cent were rehabilitated *posthumously*. Of a million party members, arrested in the second half of the 1930s only 60 to 80 thousand came back after 15-18 years of captivity. They were profoundly marked by all that they had to endure, but only very few resemble those about whom Solzhenitsyn writes today with such sarcasm.

Socialism, revolution, or religion?

In the fourth part of his book, "The Soul and the Barbed Wire", Solzhenitsyn mentions his spiritual rebirth which occurred in the camp and speaks about his return to the belief in God which had been impressed on him in boyhood but which he abandoned in his youth for the sake of Marxism. Unexpectedly the author expresses even his gratitude to the camp (though with reservation), because it was precisely his terrible ordeal that helped him to return to Christianity. *"Bless you, prison!"* he writes at the end of the chapter "The Ascent" (his italics).

In "The Ascent" he expresses some profound and bitter thoughts. But much of what he says sounds (at least to me) false. All these highly tendentious remarks about Marxism as "an infallible, intolerant Teaching" which is concerned only with material results, with material goods but "not with *Spirit*"; all these conclusions that only faith in God was saving and uplifting the morale of the inmates, while the belief in the future triumph of social justice, in a better social order was not an obstacle to moral corruption but led the prisoner practically straightway to become a stool-pigeon. All this sounds unproven and presumptious. Regretful obduracy does indeed lead the author himself into the very "intolerance and infallibility" of judgement of which he accuses Marxism. Solzhenitsyn does not consider it possible for people who are not religious to be able to tell good from evil.

Identifying socialism with Stalinism, Solzhenitsyn cannot in fact understand people for whom their ordeal, or that of their compatriots, can become a stimulus for an even more vigorous struggle for social justice, for a better future for mankind on this earth, for abolition of all the enslavement of man by man, including the pseudo-socialist forms of such enslavement. Solzhenitsyn cannot understand that socialist conviction may be the basis of a truly humanist morality. If today in Marxism-Leninism a fully satisfactory solution of ethical and moral problems has not as yet been found, this does not mean at all that scientific socialism is by nature unable to provide moral values.

Summing up his reflections in the camp, Solzhenitsyn writes:

"Since then I have come to understand the truth of all religions of the world: they struggle with the *evil inside a human being* (inside every human being). It is impossible to expel evil from the world entirely, but it is possible to constrict it within each person. And since that time I have come to understand the falsehood of all the revolutions in history: they destroy only *those carriers* of evil contemporary with them (and also fail, out of haste, to discriminate the carriers of good as well). And they then take to themselves as their heritage the actual evil itself, magnified still more."

Such a juxtapposition seems to me neither correct nor justified. One should struggle against evil in every human being, and against the carriers of evil as well as against an unjust social order. This struggle takes different forms. It is all to the good if it takes the form of a peaceful competition of ideologies, with the help of reforms and gradual changes for the better. But sometimes society has to resort to revolutionary forms of struggle which may cause victims and disillusionment, but do not necessarily lead to the increase of evil in this world. Not socialist principles alone, the teachings of any religion too can be distorted and turned against man and humanity. For this there are many examples in history, including the history of the Russian Orthodox Church, which also has its tradition of obscurantism. In the XVI century the Russian Church still burned heretics alive. Incidentally, in Stalin's behaviour and deeds one can detect not only the pragmatic attitude to coercion, to extreme measures characteristic of many revolutionaries, but also dogmatism, craftiness, intolerance, and many other features which can be traced back to his five years education in a Greek Orthodox School and three years study in the Greek Orthodox Seminary.

Solzhenitsyn paints a horrifying picture of crimes and we are at one with him in denouncing these crimes. But I still think that only the victory of a truly socialist order, of truly socialist ethical relations between men can in the long run protect humanity from a repetition of similar crimes.

Quotations from Solzhenitsyn are taken from the English edition of *The Gulag Archipelago* vol.I (Collins, Fontana) and vol.II (Collins and Harvill).

7: Solzhenitsyn's Forced Exile

On 14 February 1974 readers of *Pravda, Izvestya,* and other dailies found on the back pages of these papers a short Tass communiqué, informing them that "A.I. Solzhenitsyn has been deprived of Soviet nationality and expelled from the USSR." Who Solzhenitsyn was the Tass communiqué did not explain.

By next day all Soviet journals had already begun publishing letters, signed by leading intellectuals as well as by ordinary workers and employees, expressing approval of the decree of the Presidium of the Supreme Soviet of the USSR. People who knew nothing about Solzhenitsyn's writings or about his views were heaping foul curses and abuses on him. At the same time thousands of ordinary citizens were welcoming him in Western Europe; leaders of most Western governments were expressing readiness to grant him political asylum. Truly, "it is difficult to be a prophet in one's own country".

The Soviet press gave the impression of a quasi unanimity of views on Solzhenitsyn's expulsion. And indeed, many of those who were hypnotized by the printed word but had never read his books, believed that the abuse showered on him was justified. But there has also been a different opinion, more and more often expressed by quite ordinary people: if he is denounced, if he is chased out of the country, then surely, he must have been telling the truth.

Some of Solzhenitsyn's friends abroad, learning about the decision of the Soviet government, sighed with relief: it might have been so much worse, they said. Undoubtedly, many of our leaders also sighed with relief. They thought that at last they pulled a painful thorn out of their flesh. And although the wound will still bleed and cause anxiety, they expected it to heal gradually, and be forgotten.

Solzhenitsyn knew that he was running a great risk by publishing *The Gulag Archipelago.* He had declared that he and his family were prepared for anything. Of course, it is against the law to penalize anybody for views and opinions expressed in an artistic, scientific or journalistic work. And if Solzhenitsyn had the choice, he would have preferred imprisonment or deportation to Siberia. This, however, would have meant prolonged silence, while his expulsion painful as it is for us all and for him, does not deprive him of the possibility of further creative work. Those western journalists who predict that only spiritual death awaits Solzhenitsyn in his exile in the West are mistaken.

The expulsion of Solzhenitsyn was a moral defeat for those in authority who did not want to, and could not, answer the accusations thrown at them; neither could they make up their minds to bring him to court and judge him, not even behind closed doors. It is also difficult to see the outcome as a triumph for Solzhenitsyn: he became the victim of arbitrariness, of persecution; he lost the chance to stand on the soil of his own country, to hear around him his own language, to enjoy the company of his friends. Maybe his voice coming from Switzerland or from Norway will sound weaker than it sounded when coming from Moscow.

The Soviet government, intolerant of opposition, was not in the habit of sending its political opponents and critics abroad; it preferred simply to deprive them of their freedom (and in times past of their lives) or force them into silence by threatening their freedom or their jobs. It is quite a rare occurrence in our country for a man who preferred prison, deportation, or even violent death, to be forcibly despatched abroad. Only one such case comes to mind, namely the case of Leon Trotsky, sent first to Kazakhstan and then to Turkey.

For some time already the western press has been seeing Solzhenitsyn as "the prominent leader of the opposition". But here the similarity with Trotsky ends. Solzhenitsyn was not the head of any political grouping, of any movement or organization. And yet, through his mighty talent, unsurpassed courage, firmness of character, his uncompromising stand, Solzhenitsyn threw out a challenge to the oppression and lies of the most powerful State and, through the course of many years, conducted a single-handed struggle which was watched attentively and with anxiety by the whole world.

In 1928 Trotsky still had many followers within the country, especially among the party intelligentsia and youth. When the rumour about his possible expulsion from Moscow spread, thousands of people converged on the station, some even threw themselves across the rails. The expulsion had to be postponed and he was removed from Moscow in great secrecy.

Solzhenitsyn has probably quite a number of adherents, even though his main books have not been officially published in the country but have only circulated (in thousands of copies) in Samizdat. He succeeded in capturing a world audience; he is read by tens of millions of people of good will all over the world; one cannot simply dismiss him. His main weapon is the word, and he wields it with astonishing artistry. His fate illustrates the enormous role and potentiality of the word in our time as well as the strength of the barriers raised on the road to freedom of expression, barriers which a powerful voice could not break.

Solzhenitsyn adopted a most radical position in denouncing the political institutions and the official ideology of our country. But he was opposed to and rejected the revolutionary methods of the past and those of our time. However, by his character and temperament, by the dynamic quality of the protest which agitates him, by his single-mindedness and tenacity, by his inflexibility, he reminds me of the greatest revolutionaries of the past. Compared with him we are all modest reformers.

Personally, I do not share Solzhenitsyn's political, sociological or religious views and convictions. It seems to me that on their basis it is impossible to construe even the least tenable political and spiritual perspective for the development of our existing Soviet society towards a new morality. Yet, not only do I fully respect and understand his views; I also think that the political and moral stand he adopted allows him to see and criticize those failings which we may see only vaguely, and attack those vices with which we have grown accustomed to make peace.

The main subject of his books is the lie and the lack of freedom. As one of his friends recently remarked, it was precisely Solzhenitsyn who better than anybody else expressed what had remained unsaid by the now silent millions of those oppressed, killed, tortured during interrogations, and dead from the hardships of forced labour: and also what is not being said today by the speechless millions, deceived, frightened, or chained by all kinds of every day routines.

One Day in the Life of Ivan Denisovich and some other stories which were published in *Novy Mir* immediately became important landmarks, not only in the literary but also in the political life of the

Soviet Union. Obviously, Solzhenitsyn said in these stories no more than a small part of what he wanted to say, and was able to express later in books which have only been published abroad. Maybe he was at the time a bad strategist. But a writer and an artist often sees clearer and further than the majority of his contemporaries; this lies in the nature of realistic creativity.

Had Solzhenitsyn's books been published and freely discussed in our country, they would have undoubtedly had a great positive influence on the conscience of the whole nation. This does not mean that all his readers would have agreed with his views; nor would his writings have led the majority of the Soviet people to renounce socialism and socialist ideology. More often, such renunciation is precisely the result of persecution inflicted in the name of that ideology. The changes which occurred in our country after October are irreversible. Now we know that a violent revolution, accompanied by civil war and terror, though it benefits the country in which it occurs, also harms it. The revolution brings forth not only creative forces, and destroys not only the archaic and obsolete conventions and institutions; it also destroys many material and spiritual treasures which constitute an important heritage of the nation, valuable to men in the new society too. Abolishing the wilfulness of the former ruling classes and raising the oppressed, revolution often brings to the fore many unworthy people who perpetuate injustices and wilfulness, sometimes on an even larger scale than before: revolution also means a great social and economic upheaval, a qualitative transformation of society and a step towards a higher degree of development — it produces new realities which cannot be ignored.

But it is not true that our society is in an impasse. The Soviet Union can develop, but only on the basis of the social, economic and ideological changes that had already occurred. At present there seem to be two possible paths of such development. The first is the further strengthening of tendencies towards that barrack-like type of socialism and mute society, which are still so strong in our country. The second is the growth of democratic socialism, socialism "with a human face". Solzhenitsyn, like many of us, repudiates the first path, but does not quite believe in the reality of the second. However, his critical spirit, his courage, his talent, and his writings increase the possibility of the triumph of just such a democratic socialism.

What will Solzhenitsyn do in exile? Of course, he will write, and write first and foremost about his native country whose interest and destiny he will have at heart. As before, his books will remain important and needed, though they will henceforward reach the Soviet public by an even more complicated route; and those who will read them will run risks and expose themselves to danger.

Solzhenitsyn has not left his country for ever. It is not impossible that in a few years he will return, and we shall be able to prepare for him a respectful and friendly welcome. Good fortune will bring him back to his native country through his books, and he will rightfully take his place among the greatest of her sons.

February 1974

8: Solzhenitsyn's "Open Letter"

The *Letter to Soviet Leaders* that Solzhenitsyn has recently published is a disappointing document. But it is not difficult to argue with Solzhenitsyn on this occasion, so absurd are many of his propositions. Nevertheless, however great one's first sense of disagreement and disappointment with Solzhenitsyn's utopian and incompetent propositions, it is impossible not to perceive that his letter reflects, even if in an extremely distorted way, many problems of our society and state which are real and acute. Not everything is so simple in what we find in this new document from Solzhenitsyn's pen, and it cannot be brushed off as merely the naively self-confident discourse of a "reactionary romantic and nationalist". The attitude which is expressed in extremely sharp and even grotesque form in Solzhenitsyn's letter is characteristic of many people in our country, and this fact, in the first instance, compels us to give consideration to certain really difficult problems of the contemporary situation and immediate future.

On the National Life of the Russian People

Sakharov has already criticized, with justification, Solzhenitsyn's nationalism and isolationism. The latter writes only of *"Russia's* hope for winning time and winning salvation"* (*Letter*, p.27: my emphasis).[1] declaring that, "after all we have endured, it is enough for the time being for us to worry about how to save *our own* people" (p.19: Solzhenitsyn's emphasis). The fate of the other nations of the Soviet Union troubles Solzhenitsyn little, as we can see from one of the notes to his *Letter,* in which he treats as desirable the separation of the "peripheral nations" from the USSR, with the possible exception only of the Ukraine and Byelorussia (p.32).

I cannot share either these views or these feelings of his. But they are not chance phenomena. even though few Russians give expression to them in such a sharp way as Solzhenitsyn has done.

We are well aware, of course, that the Russian language has spread rapidly all over the territory of the USSR. The Russian people is still referred to in the press as "the elder brother". However, it is none the less a fact that the Russian people's own national life is hampered to a very much greater extent than the national lives of, say, the Armenian, Georgian or Uzbek people.

Thus, for example, Russian villages in the regions that form the centre of Russia are in an incomparably more neglected state than the villages of the Ukraine, Moldavia, Transcaucasia or the Baltic countries. Furthermore, the Russian people is in practice without a capital of its own. In becoming the capital of the multi-national Union, Moscow has almost wholly lost the features of a national Russian city, the capital of the strictly Russian lands, as it was before the Revolution. (The more Europeanized Petersburg, a city of officialdom and industry, was the capital of the Empire.) This transformation of Moscow into an international centre, deprived of its own national features, has had far from positive consequences for the Russian people as a whole.

Such a weakening of the national foundations of Russian life in the present period is neither natural nor progressive. To be sure, a partial process of integration of all nations is going on throughout the world nowadays. Some small nations which possess no old and well-developed culture are being gradually assimilated, fusing with larger nations. In most other cases, however, national culture, self-awareness and customs constitute something of tremendous value, which must be developed and cherished, in no way to the detriment of international integration in the economic, scientific and technical fields. Already before the revolution Lenin wrote that "the aim of socialism is not only to bring the nations closer together but to integrate them".[2] That was, perhaps, an over-hasty opinion. All the principal nationalities of the USSR are still far from having exhausted the possibilities of development of their national culture and national life, and it is hard to say whether this situation will change, generally speaking, at any rate in the next few centuries.

How might it be possible to facilitate not merely the preservation but also the development of the national distinctiveness of the Russian people? This is a question that calls for special consideration. Let us observe, first of all, that the proposal that was once made to separate the capitals of the USSR and the RSFSR (and a number of people were sentenced under Stalin for making this proposal) was far from being ill-founded; while extensive and urgent measures are necessary to raise the level of both agriculture and cultural life in the

Russian heartland areas, especially in the central and northern regions of the European part of the RSFSR.

Solzhenitsyn makes a different suggestion: "There is one way out for us", he writes, this is "for the state to switch its attention away from distant continents — and even away from Europe and the south of our country and make the North-East the centre of national activity and settlement and a focus for the aspirations of young people" (*Letter*, pp.31-2). By the North-East of Russia he means "the north-east of the European part and the north of the Asian part and the main Siberian massif" (p.28). "The construction of more than half our state in a fresh new place will enable us to avoid repeating the disastrous errors of the 20th century — industry, roads and cities, for example" (p.35). Solzhenitsyn proposes that there be established in the huge spaces of the North-East small enterprises based on "small-scale though highly-developed technology" (p.38) and on "the principles of a stable, non-progressive economy" (p.28). But the chief task of the settlers from European Russia would be to "set up in the wide open spaces of our North-East (at great expense, of course) the kind of agricultural system that will feed us at a natural economic tempo . . ." (p.34).

It so happens that I lived and taught for several years in a small settlement in the North-East. It was a prosperous settlement, the inhabitants being mainly workers in the nearby goldfields. Virgin forests stretched for hundreds of kilometres round about. Most households had small kitchen-gardens and some livestock. The greater part of the settlement's food supplies, however, were brought in from the South, because the whole of our zone was not very suitable for farming — the last frosts occurred in June and the first in August. This is typical of the entire North-East, the territory least well adapted to the conduct of agricultural activities, even "at a natural economic tempo". Solzhenitsyn proposes, indeed, to "thaw out" Russia's North-East, devoting to this task part of the budget for the armed forces and the whole of the expenditure on space research (p.38). Even if this were possible, however, what sensible statesman would agree to spend tens of milliards of public money on opening up to agriculture the virgin soil of the North East, when agriculture is still in such a neglected state in the regions of Surolensk, Pskov, Vologda, Novgorod, Kirov, Kaluga and Ryazan, and when reconstruction is still needed in dozens of old Russian cities — Tula,

Kaluga, Kalinin, Vologda, Smolensk, Astrakhan — where entire districts consist of rickety wooden houses that were built even before the beginning of the century? While we lack a flourishing and progressive economy in the European part of the USSR, and until we have organized a tolerable life for the whole population here, we have no right to go pioneering some new civilization or other in the North-East.

It is, of course, necessary gradually to open up the North-East, and a good deal is being done in this direction. But this cannot be an end in itself — the natural wealth of this great territory must be utilized, first and foremost, for the improvement of life in the European part of Russia, in the Ukraine, in the Baltic countries, Byelorussia, central Asia and Transcaucasia. All the republics of the USSR must take part in the opening up of Siberia's wealth, and must use this wealth to benefit their economies.

But, in any case, who would willingly agree to leave Moscow (Solzhenitsyn markedly exaggerates the burdens of life in this city) in order to live permanently in the Northern Urals or in Yakutia? Only one in a hundred Moscovites, maybe. The big cities continue to attract people from the countryside, and not only through the higher wages they offer or their theatres. We have in cities incomparably greater opportunities for intercourse with people who are close to ourselves in thought and outlook. This attraction of people towards people also plays an important part in preventing the survival of those tiny hamlets "of three cabins" the fate of which causes such distress to Solzhenitsyn.

The Position of the Orthodox Church

I do not share those of Solzhenitsyn's views which are connected with Orthodoxy. But his concern about the position of the church in the USSR is not unfounded.

It cannot be denied that the Orthodox Church was for a thousand years an important element in Russia's national life. Even today there are tens of millions of believers in our country, for whom religion is the main thing in their spiritual world. For them it continues to fulfil what are scientifically termed regulatory and communicative functions, and the function of consolation.

We know, too, that the fate suffered by the Orthodox Church after the revolution was a very dramatic one. Of course, the Church was not neutral in the fierce struggle that was waged at that time. Nevertheless, most of the persecutions that were inflicted upon it were unjustified and unnecessary. Even more regrettable were the repressions to which the Church was subjected at the end of the 1920s and in 1937-8, after which only a few hundred functioning places of worship were left in the RSFSR. The situation of the Russian Orthodox Church changed decisively for the better only during the war years and in the first decade after the war. But at the beginning of the 1960s the Church was again subjected to illegal persecution, as a result of which thousands of places of worship were closed, and many hundreds simply destroyed. Fortunately, these scandalous activities ceased after 1964. But oppression of the Orthodox and other religions and sects still goes on in various ways, and this gives rise to suffering and pain among millions of believers.

As a Marxist, I regard the Church as a survival from past epochs. I am sure that Christianity will not furnish the basis for the moral and spiritual rebirth and development of the Russian people. My hopes are bound up with the development of political freedom, freedom of speech and of information, that is, with the development of socialist democracy. However, for me the concept of this democracy also includes genuine freedom of conscience. So long as there are believers in our country, they must be allowed to perform all the rites prescribed by their religions. Oppression of the Church is also one of the ways in which democracy is violated. Encroachment, open and concealed, upon freedom of conscience in the USSR is the more inexcusable in that all the country's religious organizations have long since given up intervening in the political life of our society. In this matter Marxism ought not to copy the example given by the Church itself, which in previous centuries persistently and harshly persecuted all forms of heterodoxy.

It may be that the influence of the Church will grow in the years that lie ahead. Many people are turning to religion in an attempt to fill up the spiritual vacuum that has been formed in them. For many educated people, conversion to the doctrines of the Church forms a legal way of protesting against intensified political and ideological pressure. This presents a serious problem for an atheist state. But the state must not take the path of intensified persecution of the Church. The separation of Church and State laid down in the Constitution means that the State must not interfere in Church affairs. Believers must be given back the places of worship that have been taken from them everywhere that they request this. Permission must be granted for the building of new places of worship, especially in new industrial districts where there are quite a few believers but hardly any churches or priests. The state must refrain from interfering in the procedure for appointing, electing and ordaining clergy. The restored Church communities must themselves control Church revenues — which ought not to be subject to taxation, just as no tax is levied on donations to the Red Cross. The publishing and sale of religious literature must be facilitated. Parents who are believers must be allowed to form groups for the purpose of teaching their religion to their children. One can say beforehand that if the education provided in the schools is good, then few of these children will follow their parents' example. But this must result from free choice, and not from compulsion brought to bear from either side. Freedom must be accorded to sects — with the exception, of course, of those of the fanatical sort.

I am sure that the Orthodox Church has no future in our country. But it may continue to exist in Russia for hundreds of years yet. And if it be doomed to die, let this be a death from natural causes.

The Military-Industrial Complex and the Threat of War

I agree that the threat of war from the West has almost disappeared, although I cannot concur at all with Solzhenitsyn's view that the Western world, as a single ponderable force, has ceased to stand in opposition to the USSR. The cold war of not so long ago, which carried with it the menace of thermonuclear war, was a reality that could not be ignored. Many politicians and citizens in the Western countries might then have sincerely thought that the main threat came from the totalitarian Stalin regime. Many Soviet politicians and ordinary citizens might sincerely have been convinced that the main threat came from Western imperialism. With the equalizing of nuclear strategic potential, all these fears decreased markedly, which paved the way for detente and for the economic collaboration and exchange that consolidates this detente. These positive processes have been developing, with prolonged interruptions, since 1955, though a decisive turn toward better relations was observed only in and after 1970.

Of course, the process of detente could go faster and be accompanied by more noticeable reductions in armies and in stocks of strategic weapons. This is prevented not only by various prejudices which create distrust but also by the outbreak (not without the great powers having a hand in this) of dangerous crises in the Middle East, in South-East Asia and in Central Europe. Detente is also obviously hindered by the pressure of the military-industrial complexes both in the USA and in the USSR. The influence exerted by Soviet military and war-industry circles in the adoption of fundamental political decisions has grown since Stalin's death; it should be neither underestimated nor overestimated. I think that pressure from certain conservative military leaders will not prevent the continuance of detente, including also the vitally important problem of reducing military expenditure and cutting down strategic potentials in nuclear weapons. Already now the bulk of the Soviet divisions stationed to the west of our frontiers serve not so much as a shield against possible aggression by the Western powers as a guarantee of continued Soviet influence in the countries of Eastern Europe. An extension of socialist democracy in the USSR and in these countries would serve as a more reliable, cheaper and more effective guarantee of unity and economic and political co-operation and alliance between all the socialist countries.

More serious at the present time is the danger of war between the USSR and China. This danger, too, however, must not be exaggerated. The USSR's military-technological superiority is still so great that war would be disastrous for China especially. For this reason we may hope that neither the present leaders of China nor those who will soon succeed them will decide to provoke war with the USSR. China has still so much undeveloped land of her own that she has no need to dream of solving her population problems at the expense of Siberia. Still less can a Sino-Soviet war flare up as a result of some ideological disagreement. Military necessity ought, indeed, to stimulate in the USSR a more vigorous movement to settle people in all the regions that adjoin the frontier with China. These areas are both more suitable for human life and more suitable for agriculture than those of which Solzhenitsyn writes. But it would be unreasonable extravagance if, on grounds of the threat from China, enormous resources were to be thrown into the task of "thawing out" Russia's North-East.

I am not a military man. But it is clear to me that, in the event of war with China, Soviet armies could not carry on prolonged operations on the territory of the densely populated parts of China. Even if they succeeded in effecting a break-through to the chief vital centres of China, our armies would soon be obliged to withdraw to Soviet territory again. But neither could the Chinese army carry on prolonged operations in the scantily populated and vast spaces of Siberia, Kazakhstan and the Far East. This army, even if at first attended by success, would soon have to return to China. Therefore a Soviet-Chinese war, should such a misfortune occur, would bear very little resemblance to the Vietnam war. Such a war would develop in quite a different way from what has been forecast by Amalrik or Solzhenitsyn.

I am, however, fully in agreement with Solzhenitsyn that we must, on our part, do everything we can to avoid such a war. I agree, too, that even in the present state of our relations with China we have a sufficient reserve of strength not to be afraid of affecting a substantial reduction in military expenditure. We need to keep in mind the fact that detente in the West helps to reduce the danger of war in the East.

The Development of Socialism and Democracy

Solzhenitsyn advocates the maintenance in a future Russia of a "calm and stable" authoritarian order, for "even the will of the majority is not immune to misdirection" (p.51). While declaring himself in favour of freedom of art, literature and philosophy, Solzhenitsyn does not want, however, freedom of publication of political writings, free elections or other political liberties, for which he considers the Russian people to be unready. Essentially, Solzhenitsyn rejects for the USSR not only the prospect of social-ism but even that of democracy. Yet this is the only rational alter-native and the only possible road for real progress by all the nations of our country.

Certainly, it is impossible not to admit that the economic and social system that exists in our country is substantially different from the ideals that inspired all Russia's revolutionary parties, including the Bolsheviks. But, after all, the bourgeois society of the 19th century differed substantially from the ideals of the "Enlighten-ment" and revolutionaries of the 18th century. And it would nevertheless be unreal, in the circumstances that have been created in our country, to seek the way out by transferring to Soviet soil the economic and social structures which exist today in capitalist countries, or by returning to the national and religious values of 17th century Russia. We can proceed only from the possibilities of the society which exists in the USSR, and which is neither a state-capitalist society, as some allege, nor a society of "developed" or "mature" socialism, as is claimed by others. We can proceed only from the social consciousness which has already been formed among our people, and which will not turn either towards ancient Orthodoxy or towards capitalism. The overwhelming majority of Soviet citizens are unquestionably in favour of the socialist path of development for our society, and of no other path, even though ideas about what socialism is differ among many people. There is, therefore, no real path of development in the Soviet Union other than the perfection, in the theory and practice, of socialist society, no other path than that of transition from primitive bureaucratized variants of socialism and pseudo-socialism to socialism with a human face.

Socialism is a social system in which the free development of every individual is the condition for the development of society as a whole. This is an elementary truth of scientific socialism. Socialist society sets itself the task of securing the greatest possible satisfaction not only of the material but also of the spiritual demands of human beings. This means that in socialist countries there must be secured all the economic and social rights of the working people (in this respect the progress made in the socialist countries is obvious) and also all their political and civil rights.

For me, as for every thinking Marxist, socialist democracy means not only guaranteeing the rights of the majority but also the rights of the minority, including the minority's right to formulate and assert their own views and beliefs. Socialist democracy means guaranteeing freedom of conscience, speech and publication, freedom to receive and disseminate information, freedom of scientific and artistic creation. In socialist society there must be no persecution of heterodoxy and opposition views, for without the right to opposition no democracy can exist.

In socialist countries citizens must be granted freedom of assembly and demonstration and the possibility of uniting in associations and organizations of various kinds, including political organizations. The one-party system can only be a temporary episode in the development of socialist society. All the principal offices in State and society must be filled exclusively on the basis of free elections, in which a variety of candidates must take part. Publicity of court proceedings must be guaranteed, together with the right to defence at every stage of trial and investigation. Citizens of socialist countries must have freedom of movement within their own countries and freedom to choose their place of residence. They must have the right to emigrate and to return to their own country.

Naturally, no freedoms can be absolute and unconditional. Every one of the freedoms listed above needs certain limitations, connected with the security and rights of other citizens, social morality, and the need to safeguard State security and public order. But those limitations must be reasonable and must not be taken too far, since otherwise all real rights and freedoms will be nullified and the constitution that guarantees them transformed into a mere formal declaration.

It is also important to note that in different periods of the life of society particular importance is acquired by certain freedoms and rights of the individual. There was a time when attention had to be focused mainly on winning the right to work and to just payment, to social security, and to the abolition of social and national inequality. This period is not yet over in our country, but it has now, in my view, become much more important to win such rights and freedoms as freedom of speech and of publication, freedom to receive and disseminate information, freedom of opposition, and security for the rights of political minorities.

A very important element in democracy is, of course, freedom to emigrate. But I do not understand the logic of those who today put *this* question in the forefront and try to show that, if freedom of emigration is allowed, then the Government of the USSR will be obliged to raise the standard of living of its citizens to European levels and to allow them all the other rights and freedoms. This is all merely illusory. In Tsarist Russia at the beginning of the 20th century the right to emigrate was almost unrestricted, and hundreds of thousands of Russians, Jews and Ukrainians left their country every year, going mainly to the USA and Canada. Did the emigration help even slightly to improve the situation of the working people in Russia and to democratize the country? The same can be said of Southern Italy, Turkey and several other countries. For the majority of authoritarian regimes, freedom of emigration is even desirable, and is encouraged, since it helps, as a rule, to reduce internal tension and conflict, for thòse who leave the country are usually the least well-to-do and most discontented citizens. Freedom of emigration is the right to which authoritarian regimes can most easily consent, and this is beginning to be understood by ruling circles in the USSR.

Freedom of emigration possesses, at the present time, decisive importance only for the Jews and the Volga Germans. These national minorities continue to experience insulting discrimination, but *they*, unlike, for example, the Crimean Tatars, have a second "historical" homeland beyond the frontiers of the USSR. As regards the other nationalities of the USSR, there is no serious movement among them in favour of emigrating. A change in the internal situation in the USSR cannot be brought about through emigration but only through a struggle for democratization inside Soviet society (with support from outside, which is important for us). Any large-scale emigration by Russians, Ukrainians and Byelorussians, if such a movement were to develop, would inevitably cause bigger problems for Western Europe and the USA, and for the emigrants themselves, than for the present regime in the USSR.

Like every other Science, Marxism has the Right to make Mistakes

Solzhenitsyn repudiates Marxism, and there is no need to repeat here all the epithets he bestowes upon this doctrine. It is easy to appreciate, however, that Solzhenitsyn knows little about Marxism, for he attributes to it propositions and aims which have nothing in common with Marxism. The latter, for example, has nowhere alleged that "the proletariat . . . would never achieve anything in a bourgeois democracy" (p.42). Marxist economic theory never proclaimed that "only the worker creates values, and failed to take into account the contribution of either organisers, engineers, transport or marketing systems" (p. 42). Solzhenitsyn writes that "Marxism orders us to leave the North-East unexploited and to leave our women with their crowbars and shovels, and instead finance and expedite world revolution" (p. 45). All this is so lacking in seriousness, that it does not need refutation.

One cannot charge Marxism-Leninism with all the shortcomings and defects that still exist in the Soviet Union. For example, Marxism never declared that in socialist society there can be no individual economic initiative, and that all small private enterprises and working groups must be prohibited, including those operating in the sphere of services. Marxism bears no responsibility for the irrational centralisation of cultural life in our country, which is causing an impoverishment and enfeeblement of culture in many large cities. Marxism never stated that under socialism only one party can exist and no opposition must be allowed. Marxism bears no responsibility for the conflict between the USSR and the Chinese People's Republic. Marxist ideology bears no responsibility for the blood of those twenty-five or twenty-six million people who perished in the USSR during the years of Stalin's repressive measures (Solzhenitsyn writes of 66 million, but that is an exaggeration). Such examples could be added to.

There are, of course, in the writings of Marx and Engels and in those of Lenin not a few imprecise, one-sided and even mistaken propositions, and also some that were applicable only to a particular period of history and have lost their significance today. This is why many of Marxism's predictions have not come true, or have not been fulfilled very exactly. It remains, however, an incontrovertible fact that Marxism has had a very great influence on social and political movements of enormous scope in the 20th century, and that the entire profile of our world has been changed as a result of this – even if everything has not happened in the way the Marxists themselves would have wished. One thing is clear: that a "dead" ideology would not have been capable of inspiring and stirring to action so many people in our turbulent century.

And can any science whatsoever develop without making mistakes, without making assumptions that prove to be not quite accurate, without employing provisional hypotheses and undertaking experiments?

There are no such sciences in the field of natural science, and still less can there be any in that of social science. Marx's pupils and followers have therefore been obliged to supplement his conceptions with a number of propositions which are not to be found in his own works, and which in some cases are not entirely in accordance with what Marx himself said a hundred years ago. But this is the normal course followed by any science, it inevitably develops far beyond the circle of ideas that were worked out by the founders of the given science in their own day. In the second half of the 19th century the concepts of "Darwinism" and "scientific biology" were almost identical in content, almost synonymous. Today, however, scientific biology has advanced a long way, in breadth and in depth, as compared with the range of notions that were developed by Darwin himself in those days. But this does not in the slightest alter the fact that it was Darwin who founded scientific biology, and his teaching that served as the point of departure for its development.

Marx and Engels were the founders of scientific socialism, and Marxism remains the point of departure for the development of scientific socialism and scientific communism. But the followers of Marx and Engels cannot and must not linger within the ring of those propositions and theories alone which were worked out in the 19th century by these great thinkers. The same can be said of Lenin and Leninism.

Solzhenitsyn treats Marxism as though it were a dogma, and imagines that it is enough to point out its inexactitudes, errors and inaccurate forecasts in order to cause its followers to turn away from it. When Solzhenitsyn and I were at school, Marxism-Leninism was indeed presented to us as a dogma. But Marxism-Leninism, scientific socialism, is not a dogma but a science, which has to be developed like any other science and which has the same "right to err".

Technical and Economic Progress and the Earth's Resources

In his letter Solzhenitsyn calls for a halt to the industrial and economic progress of mankind. The teaching of the "dreamers of the Enlightenment" (p. 21) about perpetual progress has proved, in Solzhenitsyn's view, to be false and pernicious. The scientific, technical and economic progress made by man in the 19th and especially in the 20th century, progress without precedent in previous ages, and revealing the gigantic potentialities of the human mind, is for Solzhenitsyn only "an insane, ill-considered, furious dash into a blind alley" (p. 21). And the civilisation created by this progress is merely a "greedy" civilisation which "has now choked and is on its last legs" (p. 21). Solzhenitsyn writes, in capital letters: "Economic growth is not only unnecessary but ruinous" (p. 22).

He warns us that mankind is heading for inevitable doom some time between 2020 and 2070 "if it (does) not relinquish economic progress" (pp. 22-23). One cannot concur with such views – which, incidentally, were expressed by various thinkers even in the 18th century.

Of course the dangers into which mankind has run in its rapid and hitherto ill-governed advance are extraordinarily great, and much is being written about this throughout the world. To overcome these dangers, however, what is needed is certainly not to reject economic progress but rather to regulate this progress in a rational way.

Solzhenitsyn is right when he says that economic progress based on increasing utilisation of the planet's *unrenewable* resources cannot go on for long. But even if the scale of extraction of oil and gas, copper and mercury, be reduced to a fraction of what it is at present, these "useful minerals" will eventually be exhausted – if not in twenty or thirty years then in a hundred or two hundred. And yet mankind's situation is not at all so hopeless and desperate as Solzhenitsyn supposes.

There is no room here to write about all the suggestions that have been put forward in the press for a more rational utilisation of natural resources. Mankind must indeed cut down as soon as possible the use it makes of the unrenewable resources of our planet, and must also introduce stricter control over the growth of population. An extremely important line for scientific and technical progress to follow must be the reorganisation of the world's use of power supplies so as to concentrate less on coal and uranium ore (reserves of which are also not unlimited) and more on *renewable* and practically unlimited sources of energy in the first place, solar heat, subterranean heat, power from rivers, the wind, the tides, and so on. Another no less important line of technical and economic progress must be the invention of methods for maximum utilisation of all the waste products of industry and of domestic life – and this, by the way, will make an important contribution to solving the problem of pollution of the environment. Finally a third very important line of scientific, technical and economic progress must be the development and use of *substitutes,* that is, the employment in production of those varieties of raw material of which the Earth possesses a practically inexhaustible amount, in place of those substances which are in short supply and expensive. It would, of course, he possible to mention other lines of scientific, technical and economic progress as well which could help in advancing the welfare of humanity without a disastrous disturbance of the established balance of nature – for example, reduction in the weight and size of machines and mechanical devices, without any sacrifice of efficiency, partial replacement of books and journals by microfilms, and so on.

Rejecting the predatory exploitation of natural resources need not signify rejecting economic progress. Progress in agriculture can be achieved, given intelligent regulation, without exhaustion of the soil or ploughing-up of new lands, and can be accompanied, on the contrary, by an increase in the fertility of the soil. An efficient fishing industry can be organised without exterminating the world's resources in fish and with a steady increase in these resources. Mankind must thus fit itself into a well-ordered rotation of the resources and forces of nature instead of constantly disturbing this process.

Our Earth is not yet an apple gnawed away by maggots, as Solzhenitsyn thinks (p. 21). Only a small part of the skin of this apple has so far been eaten, only a very small layer of the Earth's surface. True, given clumsy and rapacious management, even this is enough to bring about irreversible and ruinous changes in the Earth's biosphere and lead mankind to catastrophe. It is quite possible, however, to prevent such a catastrophe and find a way to the rational use of natural resources without halting economic progress – through scientific control of this progress. For the potentialities of such scientific control are practically unlimited.

These aims must also be served by the various space-research programmes which exasperate Solzhenitsyn so much. Cosmic experiments can be stupid extravagances when they are carried out merely in the context of "competition" between the two systems, when they mainly serve purposes of national prestige, or military aims. But they are useful and necessary when they are carried out in a context of co-operation and for the purpose of improving man's life on Earth.

Economic progress is not superfluous or harmful, and still less is it disastrous. Such progress is inevitable and necessary for mankind. With it are bound up, first and foremost, our hopes not only for growth in the material well-being of all nations but also for the spiritual and moral progress of all mankind.

On the basic contradiction in Soviet Society

Soviet society is not free from contradictions, and these are indeed the chief stimulus to its development. It seems to me that at the present time the basic contradiction in Soviet society is the increasing disparity between the requirements of rapid scientific, technical and economic progress and the excessively centralised and, above all, bureaucratic system that governs all sides of economic and social life. The system of leadership and management that has become established in our country is incapable of solving, quickly and correctly, many problems of importance for the further development of society. Moreover, the administrative apparatus of this system tends to become isolated from the masses and is often inclined to take important decisions on the basis of its own interests as an apparatus rather than on the basis of society's interests as a whole. All this slows down progress in all spheres of the social, economic and cultural life of our people, and provides grounds for discontent and for the rise and spread of social movements of various kinds.

Our country's development cannot be accelerated unless a rational decentralisation is effected, unless the right to decide many questions is transferred to authorities at a much lower level, unless the rights and responsibilities of all local organs are enlarged, unless self-management is extended, unless public opinion is enabled to participate in the taking of decisions, unless there is free discussion of all questions of social and political life − in short, unless society is made democratic.

In the advanced capitalist countries, on the other hand, economic, scientific and technical progress demands not only that the problem of "participation'. be solved, but also that regulation by the state be extended in the economic sphere and in many other spheres of social life, including nationalisation of the most important branches of industry and all enterprises of national importance. It is significant that even an economomist like Galbraith now talks not only of planning and of nationalising the arms industry but also of socialism − although, of course, in a sense different from what we mean by this.

The increasingly acute contradiction in the USSR between the requirements of economic, scientific, technical and cultural development and the bureaucratic, caste-oligarchical system of government gives rise to an objective need for reforms directed to the democratisation of social life.

Is the present leadership of the USSR capable of introducing these reforms? Will they be introduced in the foreseeable future? I continue to hope so. In fact, the policy of the "leading circles" is changing even now, although all such changes are proceeding too slowly and inconsistently.

I am also hopeful that democratic movements of various shades will grow stronger. I do not rule out the possibility – as yet, of course, not very probable – that a new socialist party will appear in our political arena, a party different from both the present social-democratic parties and the present Communist parties. Such a new socialist party could form a loyal and legal opposition to the existing leadership and help to renovate the Communist Party of the Soviet Union and restore it to health. Not being heir to the old Russian socialist parties, a new socialist party like this could base its ideology only upon those propositions of Marx, Engels and Lenin that have stood the test of time, and also it could, not being bound by the prevailing dogmatism, develop scientific socialism and scientific communism in accordance with the needs of the present age, taking into account the historical path trodden by our country. Free from responsibility for the crimes of past decades, this party would be able to evaluate more objectively both the past and the present of our society, and would also be in a better position to devise socialist and democratic alternatives for its development. All this is, of course, no more than a hypothesis, an assumption about one possible path along which our social consciousness may develop.

I have examined above only a few of the questions raised in Solzhenitsyn's recent letter. Many of the greatest writers both of Russia and of other countries have been men of difficult character and have upheld ideological and political views that were extremely backward for their times. This has not prevented them from leaving a unique mark not only in the history of artistic creation but also in the social and political history of mankind. The phenomenon of Solzhenitsyn is in this respect no exception in world literature.

May 1974

1. Quotations from Solzhenitsyn's *Letter to Soviet Leaders* have been taken from the English translation by Hilary Sternberg, London 1974. Page references appear in brackets in the text.
2. Lenin, *Collected Works*, 4th Edition, English version, Vol.22, p.146.

9: Solzhenitsyn and Tvardovsky

I have read Solzhenitsyn's book[1] with the attention it deserves. The opening pages were of particular interest. The subject of unexpected and sudden success, of a writer's or an artist's rapid transition from complete obscurity to overwhelming and world-wide fame: this is a story dealt with in many films, which in spite of their simplicity, continue to stir the imagination of audiences.

What for millions of cinemagoers remains, as a rule, only a beautiful tale, became a reality in Solzhenitsyn's life. The main point was that he fully deserved this success; his first published novels and stories have already become landmarks not only in the development of Soviet literature, but also in the whole political and social life of the USSR.

However, as one reads on into Solzhenitsyn's new book, one's feelings soon begin to change drastically. There follows not only disenchantment, but also annoyance and regret that such a great writer should reveal so much ingratitude, such pettiness, so much injustice and lack of objectivity in his appreciation of people who in fact contributed a great deal to his literary career, and even show ill-concealed envy at the startling and dazzling success of other writers, for instance M. Bulgakov.

I cannot say how a reader who knows the people described by Solzhenitsyn only by name, will react to the book. As to myself, having known Tvardovsky so well and having been so friendly with him, and knowing also the majority of other editors of *Novy Mir,* having sometimes attended the meetings of its editorial board, I find in Solzhenitsyn's memoirs much that is not only inadmissible but also demands rebuttal.

Solzhenitsyn and Tvardovsky

Among the many people portrayed by Solzhenitsyn, the main characters are Tvardovsky and the author himself. Their first acquaintance,

their short-lived friendship, then the growing discord between
Tvardovsky, the great Russian poet and editor of our best literary
magazine and Solzhenitsyn, our greatest prose writer: this story will
always attract the attention of literary historians.

Solzhenitsyn tries to present the whole complex personality of
Tvardovsky: not only a classic among Soviet poets and a prominent
editor, but also a Member of the Central Committee of the Soviet
Communist Party, a deputy to the Supreme Soviet, and the Secretary of the Soviet Union of Writers; he was the eccentric "boss" in
whom love for Russian literature and absolute personal integrity
sometimes clashed with an equally sincere belief in the ideals of the
party and the sense of party discipline. Tvardovsky, according to
Solzhenitsyn, was a great poet, a good and upright man tormented
by the misfortunes of his country and in particular by the unhappy
lot of the muzhik; and a man who remained himself, in a sense, a
muzhik all his life. Tvardovsky was also, if we are to believe Solzhenitsyn, a great dignitary, a "general" of literature, conscious of
his proximity to the "powers of this world" and anxious to belong
to the literary "elite" and to those circles revolving at the apex of
society. One of the obvious tasks of Solzhenitsyn's work is to show
how the system of blind party discipline and hardened and dogmatic
ideology maims and mutilates as independent and strong a personality as that of Tvardovsky, and how it lays its stamp on his creativity and his behaviour. Though Solzhenitsyn clearly overstates the
tragic contradictions in Tvardovsky's personality, in this part of his
reminiscences he is indeed not too far from the truth.

But the further one delves into the reminiscences, the more one
becomes aware that the book has also another, a less noble, aim,
namely to prove that the author does not, after all, owe much to
anybody, and really owed nothing to Tvardovsky or to *Novy Mir.*

Persistently, Solzhenitsyn goes on repeating that even in the
matter of the publication of *One Day in the Life of Ivan Denisovich,*
Tvardovsky allegedly procrastinated, that he kept on delaying his
talk with Khrushchev, unnecessarily seeking the reaction to the story
of other writers like Marshak and Chukhovsky. By delaying the publication so much, *Novy Mir* "gained nothing; on the contrary, much
was lost . . . Literature could have hastened the process of history,
but it did not" and for this, as can be seen, Tvardovsky was to blame.

All these accusations are completely unjust, and in the pages which follow Solzhenitsyn himself refutes them. By the publication of *Ivan Denisovich* nothing was lost but much was gained; it speeded up the process of history; it became an important event in the political life of our country. The whole problem of publication was dealt with by all the authorities concerned with exceptional urgency; the obstacles were, however, so considerable that the final success was achieved thanks only to the extraordinary persistence of Tvardovsky who, in fact, acted by circumventing both the censorship and the Secretariat of the Writers' Union. Aware of all the difficulties, Tvardovsky showed not slowness but sensible caution. Had he acted otherwise, not only might the novel have been lost, but also all the papers and material of the author (as had happened to Grossman) as well as perhaps the author himself, at that time only a modest teacher in Ryazan.

If one were to believe Solzhenitsyn, one would think that it was precisely Tvardovsky who prevented the publication of a large number of Solzhenitsyn's works in other journals by not allowing him "to seize the crucial bridgeheads for future battles". According to Solzhenitsyn, one could, at the beginning of 1963, have published even in *Pravda* the chapters from *The First Circle* dealing with Stalin "if it were not for a *false* sense of obligation to *Novy Mir*." (My italics, R.M.)

On this point Solzhenitsyn obviously misleads his readers. Even after the 22nd Congress of the CPSU the atmosphere in the country was not such as would allow the publication in *Pravda* of excerpts about Stalin from Solzhenitsyn's novel. And if by a miracle his novels and stories did appear in *Novy Mir,* this happened precisely thanks to Tvardovsky himself. This is why it is so painful to read in Solzhenitsyn's reminiscences that although "the *Novy Mir* shackles were only secondary, they still acted as discernible drag" on him. But Solzhenitsyn himself in his letters to Tvardovsky, some of which I had an opportunity to see, wrote something *completely contrary* to what we now find in his memoirs.

From my own conversations with Tvardovsky I gathered that by defending Solzhenitsyn before the highest authorities, he was exposing himself and *Novy Mir* to danger; that he also liked him and felt hurt when Solzhenitsyn was unjustly attacked by critics or when his behaviour was worrying him. Solzhenitsyn was aware of Tvardovsky's feelings and often took advantage of them, although today he says that he more often chafed under the obdurate tutelage of Tvardovsky rather than enjoyed it: he "loved me with a pure heart and disinterestedly, but also tyrannically, like a sculptor loves his sculpture or a sovereign his vassal."

In his letters to Tvardovsky Solzhenitsyn often used to say that the most important thing was to preserve *Novy Mir*; he even suggested that Tvardovsky should distance himself from him (needless to say Tvardovsky never followed this advice). Reading Solzhenitsyn's present memoirs we see that he was greatly irritated by the fact that, with all the attention Tvardovsky was giving him, he still put the interests of his journal and its literary policy first. Indeed, it was thanks to this very literary policy that practically all the authors whom Solzhenitsyn, in 1973, called "the core of the contemporary Russian prose" appeared in print.

Today Solzhenitsyn tries to prove (and this is one more aim of his memoirs) that the editors of *Novy Mir* only deluded themselves when they thought that they stood at the centre of the country's new literary developments. Yes, he is prepared to admit that *Novy Mir* was better than other big journals. But if we believe what he says in the book, all the main currents of Russian literature were, in the 1960s, moving away from *Novy Mir* and flowing through Samizdat. The best among these uncensored writings were, of course, novels and stories by Solzhenitsyn himself. He says that he had rarely read *Novy Mir*, and that this offended Tvardovsky. As if to make amends, the author of *Ivan Denisovich* looked through 20 consecutive copies of the journal. He liked many things in it, but nevertheless he does not refrain from remarking that on the whole it should have been publishing more daring contributions, could have conducted itself more independently of the mood of the authorities, should have "got up from its knees" and paid no attention to the current political atmosphere; and that to achieve this Tvardovsky should have banged his head against the wall.

It is strange to hear such reproaches today. As a legal journal subject to censorship, *Novy Mir* could not have disregarded political circumstances and ignored the ruling hierarchy. However, the journal was not "on its knees", it did not follow directives from above blindly, but pursued its own course in a very complicated situation. Tvardovsky not only did often bang his head against the wall but sometimes succeeded in knocking it down, as in the case of Solzhenitsyn.

Solzhenitsyn relates how in 1966 he decided to submit some of his stories for publication to other journals, like *Moskva* and even *Ogonyok*. Tvardovsky viewed this almost as "treason". Trying to absolve himself, Solzhenitsyn exclaims: in truth, between *Novy Mir, Oktyabr, Moskva* or *Ogonyok* there was only a superficial difference because of the levelling effect of the "red booklet" nestling in Tvardovsky's, as well as Sofronov's and Kochetov's, left breast pocket.

The falsity of such a statement is obvious. Yes, Tvardovsky was a member of the Party. But the main lines in the struggles of the 1960s ran precisely between various currents of *socialist* thought and between different tendencies within the Party. Solzhenitsyn understood this then: he consciously concealed his own views from Tvardovsky and was, at the time, proposing to him the publication of a somewhat "trimmed" version of his novels and stories. It not only worried Solzhenitsyn that his candidature for the Lenin Prize was declined; in private talks with some writers he praised Lenin, the October revolution, and the Soviet régime at least of the early years after 1917. This was what secured for him the success of his first literary and political statements. Now, on the contrary, by adopting a strikingly anti-socialist position, Solzhenitsyn isolates himself from his former followers.

A few more words about Tvardovsky

Solzhenitsyn writes a great deal about Tvardovsky's kindness, honesty and inborn intelligence. He does not conceal his many weaknesses, indeed, in a curious way he gives his main attention precisely to these weaknesses, as if he delighted in them. He also invents vices of which Tvardovsky was never guilty.

Yes, Tvardovsky indulged in bouts of drinking. This was his misfortune, his illness, which made the difficult position of *Novy Mir* even more complicated (without mentioning that it added to his family troubles). It would be wrong to omit this fact, but it still does not merit all the attention given it by Solzhenitsyn. Describing Tvardovsky's visit to Ryazan, Solzhenitsyn, with understandable annoyance, says that already on the second day of the reading of *The First Circle,* progress began to be marred by Tvardovsky's "usual drunkenness". But why should the author of these memoirs give such a naturalistic description of the violence of the man who, allegedly, jumped up and down at night, undressed and shouted all kinds of orders, and so on? Next morning Tvardovsky remembered nothing of all this, and — adopting Solzhenitsyn's own method, one might ask: "Did this scene really occur?"

Describing his visit to Tvardovsky's *datcha,* Solzhenitsyn again writes about the beginning of another drinking bout. ". . . With heavy steps he descended from the first floor in his vest, and with bleary eyes . . .". Such incidents are repeatedly depicted, in nearly 20 or 30 pages of the memoirs: ". . . he was able to escape for two, three weeks, and on this occasion even for two months in an inconceivable alcoholic crisis . . . into a world that did not exist for his . . . colleagues but was fully real to him . . .". If Tvardovsky indeed suffered from alcoholism, many of his other failings listed in the book are only figments of a biassed author's imagination. Tvardovsky disliked the noise of traffic, which is especially loud round the many complicated street intersections in the vicinity of the offices of *Novy Mir.* Solzhenitsyn remarks: "Well, he was unaccustomed to moving about the streets otherwise than in a limousine . . ." Observing in Ryazan the awkward manner in which Tvardovsky got into a *Moskvich,* Solzhenitsyn cannot refrain from exclaiming, "In his position he got used to riding in nothing smaller than a *Volga.*" All these are pure conjectures. The first car which Tvardovsky's family acquired was a *Moskvich,* but Alexander Trifonovich was in fact too bulky a man for it. On principle Tvardovsky did not take advantage of the multitiude of privileges to which he was entitled; it irritated the other secretaries of the Union of Writers and other editors that he did not avail himself of the extra provisions available to the so-called "workers with special responsibilities". He liked walking and sometimes would go out for many hours. He would also work for hours in his garden and orchard. It is absurd and unfair to portray him as if he had been a kind of grandee, viewing the world only through the windows of a limousine.

But it is the constant talk about Tvardovsky's "lack of courage" which is absolutely shocking. Solzhenitsyn describes how he and Lakshyn went to see Tvardovsky (after the latter's month-long drinking session). He met them at the door of his home, asking fearfully: "What's happened?" "His hands trembled not only from weakness but also from fear . . ." Why "from fear"? Solzhenitsyn

himself says further that later on, when Tvardovsky was assured
that nothing wrong had happened, when he calmed down after
having dinner together, he could not manage to write a dedication
on his new book because his hands were still trembling. "I cannot,"
said Tvardovsky, "perhaps another time." Giving some further
examples – just as unconvincing – of Tvardovsky's "lack of courage",
Solzhenitsyn draws a general conclusion: "Tvardovsky was doomed
to fall into despair and drink himself silly after an unfriendly telephone call from a second rate Central Committee instructor and
equally to blossom out after a crooked smile from the director of
the cultural section".

This conclusion is just as untrue as is the remark that *Novy Mir*
was directed by "unsteady" and intermittently "weakening hands".

No, Tvardovsky was editing his journal with determination and
firmness. Of course, he had to make concessions and listen to strictures. But no other editor of any of our journals behaved with as
much dignity vis-a-vis the authorities, and none showed less servility
than Tvardovsky. Obeying instructions in small matters, he was firm
and stubborn when big issues were at stake. At one of the meetings
he raised his voice against the head of the cultural department of the
Central Committee who made a tactless remark; the official was
utterly disconcerted and unable to finish his speech. Tvardovsky
rudely silenced the secretary of the Central Committee, P. Demichev,
and demonstratively left one of the routine briefings of the chief
editors. Sometimes he was sharp and even rude in talking to L.
Ilyichev, who was Demichev's representative. And often thanks to
his pluck and rudeness the journal and many of its authors remained
safe.

Equally unjust is Solzhenitsyn's reproach that Tvardovsky allegedly always manifested "aversion to and mistrust of Samizdat". I met
Tvardovsky precisely through the Samizdat edition of my *Let
History Judge* which found its way to his desk though it was not
meant for publication in *Novy Mir*. Later on I myself very often
passed on to Tvardovsky manuscripts which were circulating in
Samizdat – he not only always read them with great interest, but he
sometimes asked me to leave them with him for his private library.
He was, however, sensible and cautious: not all material was to him
of equal value, nor did he accept the Samizdat stuff from anybody;
nor did he show the Samizdat to all and sundry, but only to his

closest friends and co-thinkers. He took great care that manuscripts officially sent to the editorial offices should not appear in Samizdat — this could have harmed greatly not only *Novy Mir* but also the authors involved.

Solzhenitsyn can deceive only those people who know nothing about *Novy Mir* when he says that not until the day of his dismissal did Tvardovsky go to the "lower floors" of the editorial offices. Incidentally, it was precisely on the "lower floors" that the main editorial work was done.

As can be seen, Solzhenitsyn is such a biassed witness that, I am sure, the ugly scene when Tvardovsky allegedly refused to accept the copy of the manuscript of *The First Circle,* the only copy saved after a police raid, is either invented or is in some way distorted, and as such it does not, as Solzhenitsyn wishes, "merit to enter literary history".

A few words about Solzhenitsyn
The Calf Butted the Oak is so full of self-praise that it borders on extreme narcissism. The author sees himself as Chosen by God and only by the Grace of God saved from innumerable dangers and temptations. Hence his "prophet complex": he sees himself, indeed, as a prophet called upon to save, if not the whole of mankind then, at least, Russia. But in the current self-adulation there also flow some admissions which can scarcely evoke sympathy. Solzhenitsyn admits, for instance, that he always concealed from Tvardovsky his own plans and his own views, and this, of course, affected their friendship.

Reading these memoirs we realize that the more open Solzhenitsyn was becoming in disclosing his reactionary-utopian ideas, the faster was he losing his former friends: he parted with A.D. Sakharov (and obviously settling his scores, he quotes many personal talks with Sakharov and his wife, talks which were certainly not meant for publication). In autumn 1973 (the autumn which he, for some reason, describes as "victorious") we see around Solzhenitsyn only a few religiously inclined young men and I. Shafarevich.

For this isolation Solzhenitsyn tends to blame everybody but himself. In the first instance he upbraids the whole of our intelligentsia for its lack of courage and spirit. Of course, our intelligentsia has many failings. But one cannot deny that we possess a sober understanding of certain realities of life which are now beyond change.

This is why our intelligentsia rejects Solzhenitsyn's and Shafarevich's religious-authoritarian vision. Solzhenitsyn's self-admiration quite often provokes only a sceptical smile, as when he says, for example, that his series of statements was not just transmitted by the news service of the Voice of America, but that "my answer . . . already thunders around the world". About his polemics in 1973 the author writes as of "battles in which helmets shone and swords resounded". Of course, the publication of *Gulag Archipelago* was a powerful blow against all Stalinists. But losing all sense of proportion, Solzhenitsyn states that it was lethal for "their" régime, that now their power will crumble.

The essential problem is, however, not how Solzhenitsyn is struggling against the authorities, but *what is he struggling for,* and what are his aims? At this point Solzhenitsyn's self-esteem becomes more and more revealing. It is not only in defence of religious orthodoxy that he has been coming forward in the last few years; but also in attacking Lenin as the villain mainly responsible for all the ills of Russia, he unexpectedly treats Stalin as a . . . "lamb": "They found a lamb," he exclaims, "to blame him for all the iniquities of communism." (Solzhenitsyn portrays himself as a calf, which also, incidentally, hardly fits the picture.)

Describing the year 1965, so difficult for him, Solzhenitsyn remarks *en passant* that one of the few joys of that year was for him the news about the failure of the Indonesian upheaval. It is, indeed, difficult to understand what joy any man who calls himself a Christian can derive from this event. The adventurist policy of some leaders of the Indonesian Communist Party and the assassination of a few generals was condemned by all communist parties. But what followed in Indonesia was a massacre of hundreds of thousands of communists and their sympathizers. For a long time the whole country was in the grip of vengeful terror and the orgy of murder extended beyond all political considerations, so much so that quite often debtors simply murdered their creditors. On the island of Bali alone, out of two million inhabitants, over 100,000 lost their lives; corpses floated all around its shores. And this terrible tragedy, unsurpassed for some two decades, brings joy to Solzhenitsyn! Here I can only repeat the words of A.F. Dementiev, whom Solzhenitsyn dislikes so much: "Can't the author be a little kinder in his attitude to people and to life?"

Some conclusions

In the preface to *The Calf Butted the Oak* the author says that apart from *belles lettres* in the proper sense of the word, there is also *secondary* literature, that is literature about literature. To this we should add that this *secondary* literature is itself of various kinds. Apart from serious and profound studies and recollections which give us an insight into men and their times (like the classical Memoirs of Herzen) there are also books dealing mainly with the private lives of writers, with their foibles, with gossip and all manner of literary scandals. Such literature enjoys great popularity among that public which lacks discrimination. It is regrettable that most of the chapters of Solzhenitsyn's book are of just such low quality.

The publication of Solzhenitsyn's first writings provoked many critical essays, some of which in themselves constituted a significant contribution to our intellectual life and gave rise to lively discussion. I should like to mention here essays by V. Lakshin and Yu. Karyakin. At the beginning Solzhenitsyn paid attention to these criticisms, as can be seen from his letters to their authors. But in his memoirs he passes in silence over such important episodes in our intellectual life. Only incidentally does he mention the stream of "unasked for" and "snivelling self-advertising" reviews, the majority of which he never read, well aware that "cockroaches" are strong. But at the same time he relates in careful detail how, at the Ryazan railway station, Tvardovsky rushed upstairs to the bar, drank half a litre without even having a snack, and already half-drunk, began the wait for the train, just repeating "Don't think badly of me."

In fact this part of the memoirs strikingly resembles those attacks on Tvardovsky and on *Novy Mir* which were repeatedly made at all sorts of closed meetings of our propaganda officials. It was precisely the employees of all grades of the cultural and ideological department of the Central Committee who used to maintain that *Novy Mir* was directed by uncertain and weakening hands, and that its editor was prone to drunkenness, as a result of which he fell under the destructive influence of some younger critics and writers. One can only deplore such a similarity of opinion.

May 1975

---

1. *The Calf Butted the Oak.* Quotations are taken from the English edition translated by M. Scammell (Collins and Harvill).

10: Solzhenitsyn and Dissent

Disagreements among the Soviet dissidents

A year ago we were still debating whether controversy among the Soviet dissidents was at all needed. Today this problem does not even arise, because the process of differentiation among them, so painful in its initial stage, has gone already too far to avoid controversy. This was quite a natural process. In 1966-68, when we witnessed the first great eruption of the democratic movement in the USSR, we were all united by the same demands: an end to the political repressions, the defence of human rights, the availability of information, an end to the discrimination against the Crimean Tartars, against the Jews, and against the Volga Germans. We were also united in our protest against the invasion by the Warsaw Pact countries of the territory of the Czechoslovak Socialist Republic, and in our criticism of the Stalinist past still persisting in many spheres of the internal policies in our country. But no opposition movement can continue for long if it bases itself exclusively on the *criticism* of an unsatisfactory state of affairs; the need for putting forward and defending some *positive* programme led, precisely, to differences of opinion and to polemics among the dissidents which we are now witnessing.

Among the currents of the intellectual opposition in the USSR I should like to mention the three most important: the movement for democratic and humanitarian socialism (the 'liberal' Marxists); the movement for the spiritual renovation of society on the basis of religion; and all sorts of nationalistic movements. Of course, there still remain other kinds of intermediate currents and interests as, for instance, groups of Christian socialists. There are those champions of the Greek Orthodox Church who are for democratization; while there are others who would rather see Russia ruled authoritatively as before. Among nationalists there are some racist elements (who speak up, for instance, against mixed marriages). Apart from all these, still continuing the fight are such a-political groups as 'Amnesty' and the Committee of Human Rights headed by A.D. Sakharov. All these groups and trends have, of course, the right to exist. However, personally, I consider as the most important and the most promising in the Soviet conditions the movement for socialism 'with a human face'.

On the 'dialogue' of the dissidents with the ruling hierarchy

A Western journalist asked me not long ago: 'How is the dialogue between the dissidents and the rulers developing at the present time?'

It seems to me that although the dissenters are scattered and not numerous, yet the Soviet hierarchy has to pay attention to them both in the internal and even the foreign policy of the country. This shows itself in its attitude towards such problems as the re-habilitation of Stalin, the emigration of Jews, Volga Germans and some others.

However, we are very far indeed from a *dialogue* as this notion is usually understood in the West; such a dialogue simply does not exist. If a 'dialogue' with the authorities occurs, then more often than not it takes the form of *an interrogation* to which practically every one of us is subjected from time to time either as a defendant or as a witness.

Democratization and public opinion in the West

Soviet society is in need of many democratic reforms, and it is obvious that Western public opinion can provide quite important support for the movement for such reforms. At present, when as a result of administrative repression, Samizdat has shrunk considerably, it is precisely the Western media of mass communication which allows the views of various dissidents to become more clearly known to our own people. For a country like the Soviet Union, the influence of Western public opinion, including its left wing, will remain helpful; but it cannot have a decisive importance. The main, the substantial change can be achieved only by the country's internal forces. For us, it is important not only to have the support of Western public opinion but to create *Soviet public opinion* which, in truth, still does not exist or is only in the first stages of its awakening.

Cooperation between governments and democratization in the USSR

Of course, agreements between governments cannot by themselves lead directly to any political and economic reforms within the Soviet

Union. Some bureaucratic methods can even be preserved by these agreements, as our propaganda gives a great deal of publicity to such successes of the administration. However, a refusal to reach such agreements and cooperation coming from our partners in the West could create an even worse situation of isolation and inadmissible pressure. This would play into the hands of the most reactionary elements in the Soviet leadership. In other words, in this respect there is no sensible alternative.

One should also consider that *in the somewhat longer run* many agreements on cooperation with other countries may become quite a weighty factor for change in the USSR, change which will depend on the extent of economic, technical and cultural development of Soviet society. Apart from this, only the establishing of a wide and solid system of cooperation and of economic inter-dependence between East and West will increase the effectiveness of the influence of Western opinion on the political atmosphere in the USSR. The Chinese Academy of Sciences can protest as long as it wishes against the persecution of dissident scientists in the USSR. Nobody will pay the slightest attention to this. If our attitude to the protests of American scientists is immeasurably more serious, this is due mainly to the fact that Soviet scientific establishments cooperate with the American ones on a series of important projects. And this cooperation is precisely the result of official agreements between the two governments.

On the pressure of the Soviet Union on Western countries

Economic sanctions as a method of pressure on the foreign or domestic policy of any country are, as we know, adopted as a system even by the United Nations Organization. The British government to this day applies sanctions against Rhodesia, and the United States against Cuba. The European Economic Community applied economic pressure on the military-dictatorial régime in Greece. In 1973-74 the Arab countries quite effectively used oil as a weapon against the West.

In the past the Soviet Union too resorted quite often to this method, refusing, for instance, to trade with Spain, Portugal, Greece, the United Arab Republic, Israel, and later on, with Chile. In his time Khrushchev tried to exert economic pressure on China, recalling from there all of a sudden all economic advisers and specialists, which forced the Chinese to abandon work on many important projects. The advantages or disadvantages of economic sanctions always depend on the concrete situation: sometimes sanctions can indeed bring about the desired changes in the policy of a given country; but sometimes they only harden and preserve the existing reactionary regimes.

Of course, many-sided economic cooperation between the USSR and Western countries creates the possibility not only of Western pressure on the Soviet Union but also of pressure by the Soviet Union on Western countries. There is no doubt that in certain circumstances our country will resort to the same methods. This is quite often used as an argument against economic agreements with the USSR. I do not regard this argument as a decisive one. After all, economic cooperation and trade are practically always conducted on the basis of *reciprocity*. In other words, cooperation benefits not only the Soviet but also the Western economy. This is why one should, of course, reckon with the possibility of Soviet pressure on the West, but this should not, by any means, constitute a sufficient reason for refusing to enter into economic cooperation. However, it should be understood that even the most profitable commercial agreements between governments and private business should not stifle a critical approach from public opinion.

The strengthened international situation of the USSR and the weakened position of the West

If in the second half of the 1960s the international situation of the USSR was continually worsening, in the first five years of the present decade we are witnessing a contrary phenomenon: we see a gradual strengthening of the international position of the Soviet Union and of its influence abroad. This is a result not only of changes in many aspects of Soviet foreign policy which undoubtedly has become more flexible than it used to be (the so-called peace offensive of the USSR). The fact is that Western countries have suffered in the last few years a whole series of painful failures in their relations with the 'third world', failures from which the Soviet Union was able to derive quite considerable advantages. Growing economic difficulties and internal contradictions between Western countries (for instance the conflict in Cyprus) also weaken the position of the West.

The Soviet Union was able to derive considerable advantages from the successes of the forces of the Left, which compensated

by far for the Chilean defeat. However, one gets the impression
that the most reactionary part of the Soviet leadership is interested
in victories of Left and communist forces only in relatively small
countries of the West which puts these countries into a state of
economic and political dependence on the support of the Soviet
bloc. This reactionary part of the Soviet leadership is not really
interested in (rather it fears) victories of Left forces in the major
Western countries which might become an independent centre
of attraction for democratic and left-wing movements. This became particularly noticeable last year during the Presidential campaign in France.

Anyhow, the weakening position of the West, and especially
of Western Europe, which has occurred in recent years, should
obviously serve as an additional stimulus for a movement of unification of Western European countries into a more tightly knit
European economic and political community. In the last analysis,
this process of unification is, from the socialist point of view,
progressive regardless of the present capitalist forms of such unification. This is why I do not understand the attitude of those groups
on the socialist Left which adopt an isolationist and nationalist
position rather than an internationalist one. Until now the proletarian movements and proletarian organizations in Western Europe
have shown much less ability to unite their forces than have all
kinds of bourgeois-monopolistic organizations and groups.

The gradual process of unification of Western democratic countries not only creates better conditions for peaceful socialist transformation (for instance, by the enlargement of the nationalized
sector of the economy), but constitutes also an important barrier
against the development of reactionary political tendencies in the
Soviet Union.

If today the Soviet Union is, in the first instance, in need of
an enlargement of democratic rights, of freedom, and a series of
democratic political reforms, then the West, because of the development of the economic crisis, is in need of sensibly devised social-
economic changes. Today that much is understood also by many
bourgeois economists (Galbraith and others). The unification of
precisely these outwardly different trends can become the foundation on which a viable and flourishing community of nations
can be built on our planet.

According to the old legend, the King of Gordium in Phrygia rode up to the temple in a carriage. An oracle declared that whosoever succeeded in untying the strangely entwined knot which bound the yoke to the pole should reign over all Asia. Alexander the Great, according to the story, simply cut the knot by a stroke of his sword. Political, economic, domestic and other problems of big and small nations are now tied up into more complicated knots than the Gordian one; but nobody would now cut through the knot with the weapon of war. On the contrary, the main international problem consists in this: that under no conditions should the weapon of war be used. There is only one way: gradually, consistently, armed with patience and determination, to untie one after another the knots of our contentious problems. In this the development of many-sided economic and cultural cooperation can be useful, not a return to confrontation and the cold war.

Is the Soviet leadership capable of making changes?

It is well known that the doctrine of Marxism-Leninism or of scientific communism justifies the use of force and the violation of many democratic rights only for the comparatively short period of the immediate revolutionary transformation of bourgeois society. But once socialism is victorious — and our propaganda maintains that we have already entered the period of 'mature' socialism — full democracy and all the democratic rights of the individual must be guaranteed in a manner that should be incomparably better than this was possible under capitalism. Unfortunately, in this respect our performance still falls very far short of the requirements of our own ideological doctrine.

It is incorrect to ask, as Western correspondents in Moscow frequently do, 'How far can Soviet communism go towards liberalization in the field of human rights without violating the requirements of Marxism-Leninism?' It would be more correct to ask the question in a different way: 'how capable is the Soviet leadership of introducing democratic reforms within the framework of socialist society and of getting rid of the various elements of pseudo-socialism and pseudo-communism?'

Even within socialist circles in the West many people imagine that there is complete uniformity within the Soviet establishment both as regards the Soviet system as well as its management which is said to operate without any 'feedback'. This view is schematic and false. Of course, the Soviet establishment is united by a mass of material and other privileges which it holds on to tenaciously. But nevertheless it is not uniform, and it would be a mistake to think that our leaders do not realize what is going on 'down below' among the working-class, the peasantry, and the intelligentsia. Their reaction to it is something else again.

Of course, because we have no free press or opposition, because political minorities are denied the right to free speech and free assembly, our country is deprived of many of the most important channels for 'feedback' and this weakens the influence of society on the policies of the leadership. But in one form or another 'feedback' exists in our system of government. And the leadership knows what is going on much better and more accurately than we, as ordinary Soviet citizens, do. We have no access to the official and secret information which includes an enormous amount of data which would not be considered secret in the West, beginning with the number of people killed and injured in industrial accidents and going on to the annual number of abortions performed on schoolgirls. As for the majority of shortcomings in Soviet life, including separate outbursts of mass dissatisfaction among workers in the provinces, the Soviet leadership is much better informed than the rank and file. We scientists, even though we specialize in social science, are no exception and our data about the processes going on in the country are too fragmentary and superficial.

With all their privileges the Soviet leadership is still subjected to quite a strong influence from below. By a whole variety of channels popular demands particularly in the economy penetrate to the very top, not to mention the growing tensions caused by economic competition with the capitalist countries. But all these influences from below and from abroad produce no single or uniform reaction in the leadership.

In the present leadership of the Central Committee of the CPSU there are nowadays no proponents of authoritarian government. Solzhenitsyn's worries about the rapid democratic changes demanded by Sakharov are completely groundless. One can clearly distinguish three main trends within the leadership.

The first of them is represented by a group of reactionaries, led apparently by Mikhail Suslov. They want a stiffening of internal policy. They are against any rapprochement or cooperation with their capitalist neighbours. In fact they would like to move backwards to a restoration of a slighty revamped form of Stalinism. In the ideological field typical representatives of this group are people like Trapeznikov and Yagodkin. Needless to say, a victory by this group in the inner-party struggle which has sharpened in recent months would have catastrophic consequences.

In the second group one can locate the more moderate politicians, whose main slogan over the last ten years has been 'stability'. Stability was what the Soviet establishment wanted. They were tired of the numerous changes and reforms of the Khrushchev era and were still quaking from the horrors of Stalin's terror, against which no-one was secure. It was this that guaranteed the victory of the more moderate section of our leadership, Brezhnev, Andropov, Grechko, Gromyko, Kosygin, and Podgorny, over the Suslov group and the Shelepin and Semichastny group who were the main organizers of Khrushchev's dismissal.

It is impossible to deny that this group in the last five to six years has achieved certain successes, particularly in foreign policy but less so internally. But progress in many fields, especially the economy, was too slow and the need for changes has grown so much that the slogan 'stability' has now become a brake on our society's development. This has produced a significant strengthening of the so-called 'technocrats' within the leadership. These are the comparatively younger leaders, who want to modernize the management of the economy and science, and would like closer links with the West and a more tolerant internal policy. These people are without many of the prejudices and complexes of the older generation, and they are capable of bringing in reforms which, even if they will not change the basic face of our society, will open a wider road to progress and democracy.

There are nowadays quite a few of these people around Brezhnev, both among the leaders of the various union republics and area committees, and among the secretaries of the central committee and the ministers and their deputies. In the coming years and even months much probably depends on a possible alliance between these technocrats and the main representatives of the 'moderate' group.

Precisely because we have no democratic system of leadership, the role of individual personalities is especially great even though this perhaps does not fully agree with Marxist doctrine. Every serious historian must be aware that if in 1917 the leader of the Bolsheviks had not been Lenin but Kamenev, as it was developing before Lenin's arrival from Switzerland, then the October Revolution would not have occurred, but instead there would have been a Constituent Assembly with a strong Bolshevik faction. If after Lenin the head of our party had not been Stalin but Bukharin, then there would not have been collectivization in the Stalinist form nor the terror of the Thirties and Forties. And if after Stalin's death Beria or Malenkov had emerged at the head of the party, there would have been no Twentieth Party Congress and no Twenty-Second Party Congress, nor that mass liberation of political prisoners about which even Solzhenitsyn writes as though it were the result of a 'spiritual impulse' of Khrushchev's. So it is impossible to be indifferent about the possible changes in the Soviet leadership and think that détente will go on regardless of who becomes head of the CPSU and the USSR in the next few years.

Liberalizing emigration and the prestige of the USSR

I have often been asked recently 'How can an inter-governmental plan for emigration from the USSR be worked out which will save Moscow's face?'

First of all, I think that even if the Soviet Union's frontiers were fully open, there would be no massive emigration; the capitalist countries themselves would not allow it. Unfortunately our authorities consider that any significant emigration from the country 57 years after the revolution would be 'a loss of face'. In his time Lenin said that considerations of prestige have no importance for the Soviet state and that when it comes to prestige issues 'we are quite indifferent and ready to ridicule them' (*Collected Works*, 5th ed., Vol.45, page 239). This prediction however did not come true and the USSR like most other states remains highly sensitive to prestige issues. That is why the US Congress and any other Western state institution has much less influence than Western public opinion.

When he produced his famous Amendment two years ago, Senator Jackson thought he would get from the USSR certain concessions towards freer emigration. But the Senator did not know how to maintain enough political tact and reasonable flexibility, as a result of which the USSR repudiated the 1972 trade agreement, even though it was very useful for both sides. As a result it was Jackson himself who lost face, all the more so since Jewish emigration is currently running at the same rate as in 1974. Senator Jackson thought he could prove his great influence over the Soviet Union as well as his personal influence in the Senate. He forced the American and Soviet leaders to take account of his views. This was in itself a great achievement. But he then went on to make himself look like the old woman in Pushkin's story about the Fisherman and the Fish, and he ended up with a broken trough. The insulting remarks about me which Jackson made when he announced his candidacy for the Presidency (*New York Times*, 28 January 1975) only testify to his short temper and inability to learn the lesson of a political failure.

The 'new' emigration and the democratic movement in the USSR

Neither the wave of emigration from Russia before or after the Revolution, nor the so-called 'non-returners' in 1945 and 1946, in spite of their size (each wave consisted of between two and three million people) had practically any effect on the life and development of Soviet society. Even simple correspondence with relatives was impossible for decades. Russian life, Russian organizations, and the Russian émigré press abroad were complete unknown to us. Only at the end of the 1960s when Soviet samizdat trickled out abroad did we learn of certain Russian journals and newspapers where these articles were reprinted and commented on.

It is quite different now with the present wave of Russian and Jewish emigration. A significant part of this emigration consists of people who are well-known in the various circles of the Soviet intelligentsia. Many of them are people well-known in the West and for that reason their opinions, statements, and arguments are listened to with attention on both sides of the Soviet frontier. Only time will tell how far the new Russian emigration uses the advantages of its position.

So far we see that with all their differences of opinion, at times very sharp, most of the new émigrés continue to live for their motherland. Undoubtedly this allows the best representatives of the new emigration to make a contribution towards the development of the democratic movement in Russia, possibly an even bigger contribution than they could make when they were here.

About the attitude of the dissidents in the Soviet Union to Solzhenitsyn

Today in all Soviet dissident circles, and indeed in the whole thinking section of the Soviet intelligentsia, people listen to Solzhenitsyn with attention and respect. *The Gulag Archipelago,* obviously, arouses the greatest interest. In spite of all the shortcomings of the author's conception, it will always remain the greatest testimony to the terrible tragedy our people lived through.

If however many dissidents now have a different attitude towards Solzhenitsyn, this is not because he now lives in Switzerland but mainly because of his own political and religio-political statements. The notorious 'Letter to Soviet Leaders' which he published a year ago undoubtedly disappointed most dissidents. And many objections were called forth by his remarks in an interview in Zurich and Stockholm in November and December 1974 which only the Russian language journal *Russkaya Mysl* published in the West. And the collection of essays by Solzhenitsyn and Shafarevich, called *From Under the Rubble* produced a decisive protest by most readers among the dissidents. I must say with sorrow that in the recently published book in Paris, *The Calf Butted the Oak,* Solzhenitsyn distorted the picture of Tvardovsky, who is dear to me and to us all, not to mention his comments about other editors of *Novy Mir.* Solzhenitsyn also writes with insulting disdain about Sakharov. Besides this Solzhenitsyn reproduces in his book many private, even intimate conversations with Tvardovsky, Sakharov and others. These conversations were never intended for publication and in many instances their contents have been distorted. Of course in the book Solzhenitsyn's artistic genius shines forth in all its brilliance. But when I read each new book or statement by Solzhenitsyn I frequently ask myself 'Is he not one of those great artistic people whose talent far surpasses his intellect?'

In the twentieth century Russia has given the world many geniuses. We have had not a few people who acted or wanted to act as prophets. But the conjunction of the powers of a genius, strength of will, and the complex of a prophet have only come together three times in the last hundred years: with Tolstoy, Lenin and Solzhenitsyn. But it is clear that the main thing for Solzhenitsyn remains his work as a writer and not his political activity. As a writer Solzhenitsyn will always be one of the very greatest of Russians. But as a prophet he will have far fewer followers than Tolstoy.

From Under the Rubble

I personally cannot but welcome the rebirth of a free Russian press of various tendencies, even though it is published abroad. How regrettable, however, that the free expression of thought by authors published outside the Soviet Union is not accompanied by a deepening of thought; that the inquiry into the most important problems is conducted on such low levels that any serious debate is impossible; the lack of tolerance of differing viewpoints comes again to the fore, together with narrowmindedness and dogmatism, which in the last analysis are analogous to a 'party line' of the worst kind though with a new content. Solzhenitsyn, for instance, writes in his first essay: 'For decades during which we were silent our thoughts straggled off in a hundred different directions, never hailing each other, and so failing to get to know each other, and so never to correct each other. The shackles which constrained our thoughts maimed all of us, leaving hardly any brains undamaged . . . and now, even when minds that are strong and brave try to stand up straight, throwing off that pile of crazy rubbish, they still bear the marks that were branded upon them, still suffer from the crookedness of those lasts on to which they were forced when immature – and owing to their intellectual isolation from one another, they cannot test their ideas against anybody else.' (*From Under the Rubble*, p.8, Paris 1974.)

There is a great deal of truth in this. But why is this description directed first and foremost against A.D. Sakharov, when it is precisely Solzhenitsyn himself and his co-authors who suffer from one-sidedness, from a tendentious subjectivity imprinted on their minds?

In the first essay of the volume, Solzhenitsyn, pronouncing on the 'deadly sins' allegedly committed by political democracy in recent years in the West, advocates the re-introduction in Russia of an authoritarian-theocratic regime, of the *non-party* or *partyless* (Solzhenitsyn's italics) rule of a 'spiritual elite', and adds that 'the ways and principles of creating such an elite and of its functioning can have very little in common with contemporary democracy' (p.23). But is it not clear that such a regime will be nothing but a dictatorship, precisely a dictatorship of the least influential *party* of our society?

The authors of the essays, contained in *From Under the Rubble*, especially Solzhenitsyn and Shafarevich, not only do not accept socialism and the socialist idea — they are full of hatred of social- ism and are unscrupulous in the mode of their struggle against their opponents. The almanack *The Twentieth Century* already con- tained some essays criticizing the religious-ethical projects of Sol- zhenitsyn, Shafarevich and their co-authors. As to their socio- political and economic pronouncements, there is simply no basis for scientific debate. For example, I. Shafarevich, criticizing Marx- ism, devotes a great deal of attention to the fabrication according to which Marx and Engels defended . . . the common possession of wives as an important socialist idea. It may be worth mentioning that in his article on principles of communism Engels, answering the 'lamentations of the highly moral burghers about the common ownership of wives under communism' wrote: 'Community of wives is a peculiarity of bourgeois society; it is brought to its highest point of perfection by the community of women called prostitution. Prostitution is rooted in private ownership: destroy the latter and prostitution disappears. Far from inaugurating an era of the common ownership of women, a communist organization of society puts an end to such a condition of things.' (K. Marx and F. Engels, *The Communist Manifesto*, p.336, London 1930.) In other, later writings (*The Origin of Family, Private Property, and the State*) Engels again showed how in socialist society the family would become more healthy and more stable than it had been under capitalism, and devoted quite a few pages to this. How can there be any basis for a discussion with Shafarevich!

Both Solzhenitsyn and Shafarevich are trying to maintain (with- out however adducing any proof) that in bourgeois countries 'from the beginnings of industrial production', capitalists do not exploit workers, but, on the contrary, the workers, as a result of successful strike action, 'are receiving an increasing part of the product which *they do not produce*'. (Underlined by Solzhenitsyn, p.10.) In other words, the workers exploit the engineers, the scientists, and the very capitalist-managers of the enterprises. How can there be a basis for any serious debate here!

Objecting to the socialist principle of *equality*, Shafarevich does not quote the famous words of Marx and Engels on how, after the victory of socialism 'in place of the old bourgeois society with its classes and class antagonisms, there will arise an association [of free producers] in which the free development of each will become the free development of all'. Shafarevich does quote, however, the crazy reasonings of one of the characters from Dostoyevsky's *The Possessed* about the destruction, under socialism, of all genius, all talent, about the lowering of the level of education, and so on, and so forth. How can there be any basis for a scientific discussion here!

In his preparatory work for *The Holy Family,* Marx took a number of excerpts from the writings of his opponents and his precursors in the camp of the so-called petty-bourgeois, bourgeois, and feudal socialism. Copying these excerpts from Marx's notebooks, Shafarevich names Marx himself as 'the author of these brilliant thoughts'. How can there be here any basis for polemic!

Referring to some rather controversial ideas of Freud on the death instinct which allegedly dwells in every one of us, and also quoting a song popular during the first years of Soviet régime, 'We shall courageously fight for the power of the Soviets, and *as one shall die*', Shafarevich at last comes to his main them: 'Life fully permeated by socialist ideals must lead to the universal result: *the dying off of the whole of humanity, its death.*' (p.66) And further: '*To the immanent forces influencing the course of history belongs the yearning for self-destruction, the death instinct of humanity*'. And it is precisely 'socialism, which takes possession and subordinates to itself millions of people, which constitutes this movement and its ideal goal: the death of humanity.' (pp.69-70) (Shafarevich's italics).

It makes no sense to argue against such statements and prophecies, because they are not rooted in the logic of scientific analysis but in the emotions. In his article Shafarevich maintains that socialism not only threatens the very existence of humanity, but also paralyses its most hopeful weapon, namely the mind. But we see that his own mind is already paralysed to a considerable degree not by socialism, but by his blinding hatred of this one tenet which in truly scientific form can save humanity from many dangers really threatening it.

Kontinent

In principle we can only welcome the appearance of *Kontinent,* a new journal which widens the margin of free discussion about contemporary topical problems. In any case, I have read with interest the two copies of the journal, though I do not share its ideological platform. However, on reading *Kontinent* one becomes clearly aware that the journal is addressing itself in the main not to the East but to the West, and that its principal task is to turn Western intelligentsia and youth against Marxism and socialism. It is quite clear that the aim of the founders of the new journal was to supply anti-communist and anti-Marxist western ideologues and publicists with new squads of professional writers and publicists from the USSR and Eastern Europe who as eye-witnesses, so to say at 'first hand', unmask not only certain perverted forms or 'models' of socialism, but socialism and communism in general. It was therefore perfectly natural and logical for Maximov to turn for support to the Springer concern. The claims made by Ionesco about the creation by *Kontinent* of a new Left ideology of which the West is allegedly in great need, are simply ridiculous and absurd. It was certainly not for the benefit of the Left that the new journal was founded. Its editor Vladimir Maximov not so long ago was still a close collaborator and protégé of V. Kochetov, for years the leader of the Stalinists in matters of literature.

I am convinced that the Western Left, including Marxists, have enough opportunity to reply to the challenge of *Kontinent*. A discussion would certainly help in clarifying many important points.

As far as the artistic side of *Kontinent* goes, there still remains a lot to be desired. The novel of V. Kornilov *Without Hands, Without Legs,* was written some ten years ago and is not the best of his prose works. V. Maramzin's *The Story of Ivan Petrovich's Wedding* did not seem interesting to me. N. Korzhavin's *Essay in Poetical Autobiography* has been circulating a long time in typescript in the Soviet Union, but has not proved a great success in Samizdat.

The article by A. Sinyavsky *The Literary Process in Russia* is too superficial, though it contains some important reflections. The memoirs of Cardinal Midszenty, published earlier in the West, have not aroused the interest of the Soviet readers of *Kontinent*. To me the most serious article seemed to be that by L. Kolakowski *Three Main Strands in Marxism* and D. Anin's *Is Bukharin Topical?* These writings at least permit a discussion with the authors on a sufficiently high professional level which, unfortunately, cannot be said about the obdurate essay by Solzhenitsyn on *Sakharov and the Letter to the Leaders* (no.2).

However, the worst material in *Kontinent* comes from the pen of its Editor-in-Chief, Vladimir Maximov. And it is not a question of his views or of his attitude, but of his conscious falsification of well-known historical facts. Already in the first editorial of the first copy of *Kontinent*, Maximov wrote that 'in the dark epoch of reactionary Tsarism there came into being a Russia, and there developed *without hindrance,* one of the greatest literatures of mankind. In these times of "slavery" nobody . . . had to look for a publisher abroad. All authors of some prominence, we are under-lining *all,* were published in their country.' (*Kontinent*, no.1, p.3). But all this is obviously misinforming the Western reader. Wasn't Radishchev exiled to Siberia for his *Journey from Petersburg to Moscow*? Wasn't it from his suicide that our XIX century litera-ture began? And the destruction of Rileyev, the exile of Kukhelbek-ker, the deportation of Shevchenko, of Chernyshevsky, the forced labour of Dostoyevsky, were they not the result of 'political con-siderations'? And was Griboyedov's *'Tis Folly to be Wise* published during the lifetime of its author? Wasn't one third of Pushkin's poems secretly circulated in manuscript till the author's death? Can one explain the suicidal death of Pushkin and Lermontov in duels by private reasons only? And the emigration of Herzen and Ogarev, and the whole epos of the *Polar Star* and *The Bell*? And the death of Polezhaev? Not long ago the libraries of Moscow and Leningrad made a list of those many hundreds of artistic works by Russian writers which were banned by the censorship in the XIX century and could only appear abroad. Not a few of Tolstoy's writings cir-culated secretly in manuscript and first saw the light of day in Europe.

In No.2 of *Kontinent*, in the 'Editor's Column', Maximov writes, addressing himself to Left-wing groups in the West: 'Certain circles — with a flourish worthy of a better cause — have recently provoked a hysteria about repressions in Chile (two thousand prisoners!) . . . What would these zealots of freedom and humanitarianism say, for whom and in the name of what will they stir up the whole world now, when all, we repeat all, political prisoners in Chile have already been released.' (no.2, pp.468-469). The clamour and insistence with which Maximov repeats this well-known lie is indeed worthy of a better cause. Of course, the defence of Soviet writers and Soviet dissenters against political repression (it is with this that Maximov begins his Editor's Column) is an important and noble action. But why should one at the same time minimize or even justify inhuman repressions in Chile and in some other countries of Western Europe? Such deliberate bad faith can in no way benefit *Kontinent*; it will only repel prospective contributors-oppositionists from both inside the USSR and outside it. This makes me think that with an editor like Maximov the failure of the journal is unavoidable.

Against the new messianism

Of course, the experience of Russia and the USSR is very great and other countries must take account of it. In addition that experience was gained at too high a price. But it is in no way Universal, and we are the ones who must make it primarily our own, here in our own country. And if it is right to reject the view that the solution of Soviet problems can come from outside as a result of foreign pressure, then it is even more necessary to give a decisive rejection to the attempt to revive a new form of Russian messianism: that is the view put out by some groups of Russian dissidents who say that only Russia because of all its suffering in the twentieth century can show the world the true way. On the jacket of the first issue of *Kontinent* there appear Solzhenitsyn's words that 'the intellectuals of Eastern Europe speak with the combined voice of suffering and knowledge' and that Western Europe will soon meet its own sorrow 'if its ear remains indifferent'. But has not Western Europe in the twentieth century gone through the terrible experiences of two world wars, several revolutions, the fascist 'New Order' with its totalitarianism, its genocide and its gas chambers, and the experience of several bloody colonial wars? Why cannot Europe find the solution to its own problems, without repeating Russia's mistakes?

How much of this self-confident messianism appears in Shafarevich's articles? 'Russia's way of resurrection is the one on which mankind can find the way out of the impasse, find salvation from the mad race of industrial society, the cult of power, and the gloom of unbelief. We are *the first* to have reached the point where *the uniqueness* of this way can be seen. It is up to *us* to set off along it and *show it to others* . . . The past half century has enriched *us* with an experience *which no other country in the world has had* . . . Russia's position is this: it has gone through death and can hear the voice of God' (*From Under the Rubble,* Pages 275-6. My italics — RM). These attempts by Shafarevich, Maximov, and Solzhenitsyn to set themselves up as mankind's teachers seem bound to fail.

One should not ignore the real situation

How do Shafarevich, Solzhenitsyn and their sympathizers propose
to solve our difficult problems and cure society's social ills?

'The way to freedom', Shafarevich writes, 'begins inside ourselves, by stopping the climb up the ladder of careerism and the
search for material well-being' (*From Under the Rubble,* page
269). Any Marxist revolutionary can agree with this. The question
is *why* should a person give up his material well-being. Shafarevich
believes you should do this not for the sake of art or literature
or scientific knowledge because even without all the millions of
experts and expensive laboratories it is possible to get to know
'the divine beauty of nature' and the 'divine design'. Solzhenitsyn
and Shafarevich maintain that society's social ills can only be healed
by religion, that only Orthodoxy can lead the way to freedom,
and that only thanks to the Church should one make sacrifices.
'One must not forget', Shafarevich writes, 'that sphere of culture
which can be more important than all others for a nation's healthy
existence — religion . . . Probably here is the key to the question:
Russia's life, death, or resurrection depends on the efforts made
in this field. This is our people's most important field of activity
and it demands hundreds of thousands of heads and hands. Let us
remember that before the Revolution Russia had 300,000 priests.
And of course the only people who can work on this today are those
that have renounced the system of values which life offers them now'
(*From Under the Rubble,* pages 271-2).

Remembering that the collection *Landmarks,* whose spiritual
descendants the authors of *From Under the Rubble* call themselves, was repudiated by the entire Russian intelligentsia from
the Cadets to the Bolsheviks, Solzhenitsyn does not expect the
present generation of the Russian intelligentsia to be more con-
descending towards *From Under the Rubble.* So in advance he
calls our entire intelligentsia despicable, stupid, cowardly, soulless
and sunk in the worries of the petit bourgeoisie. It is not an intelligentsia but only 'a superficially educated group'. The 'central' version of this group is how he describes the Moscow intelligentsia for
whom Solzhenitsyn has a special hostility. In spite of its great

material privileges and high level of information it continues to cringe before the authorities, he says. Solzhenitsyn sees no hope in a few small groups of religious young people, round which the shape of new structures may begin to form as though round tiny crystals. All these views are nothing but Utopian.

Of course, our intelligentsia has many faults, but also many achievements to its credit which the intelligentsia at the turn of the century did not and could not have. It consists of not only the leading section of our society but a rapidly growing and influential one. Without its active participation no serious changes in Soviet society are possible. But in order to arouse it to action, you have to start from its real position, its real interests and its present view of things.

Expressing his hope for miraculous changes in social awareness, Shafarevich recalls 'the unknown monk Luther' who 'took up the fight against the mightiest power in the world of that time, and apparently went against all social and historic laws'. (*From Under the Rubble,* page 263.)

But no. Luther did not act against all social and historic laws. His fight four hundred years ago was not against the church and religion, but for reforms within the existing Christian church, for a renewal of its rotten structures and against the disgraceful practice of selling indulgences. Already the vast majority of German society of that time was ready to accept Luther's ideas, and precisely because of this Luther's popularity and influence grew unexpectedly rapidly even within the aristocracy. But Russia at the end of the 20th century is not Germany in the 16th century and our people remain for the most part indifferent to the religious preaching of Shafarevich and Solzhenitsyn, just as the burghers, peasants and princes of 16th century Germany were indifferent or even hostile to the preaching of the atheists. The only chance of success with our intelligentsia or the working class lies with preaching that is based on the demand for reform, and not on the rejection of socialist society. No-one can turn Russia or Europe back to the 16th century.

April 1975

11: The Distribution of Evil

More than 100,000 people have emigrated from the USSR to the West in the last four to five years. People have left for a number of reasons. In some cases their departures were forced ones, while in the case of Alexandr Solzhenitsyn it was an outright deportation. A few individuals have been allowed to travel abroad and once there, the Soviet authorities have prevented their return by depriving them of their Soviet citizenship and confiscating their passports. This stream of emigration, which began with the strictly Jewish emigration. Incarcerating the dissidents in prisons and psychiatric establishments at first provoked prolonged and powerful protests in those democratic countries in the West, with which the Soviet Union wanted to improve its relations. On the other hand, allowing dissidents to emigrate to the West met with the approval of the West and was the result, to some extent, of pressures exerted by the West. Consequently, parallel to the Jewish emigration, there has been a continuous, even if tiny, rivulet of Russian, sometimes even religio-nationalist emigration of Russian Orthodox believers, who wasted no time in joining the anti-Soviet campaigns in the West by bringing them their own recipes for "saving" the West from the Communist threat and by offering their own methods for changing the situation inside the Soviet Union.

In this wide spectrum of voices from the new Russian emigration, Alexandr Solzhenitsyn's voice is of special weight, principally because among the people banished in the last few years from Russia to the West he is the greatest and best known figure. His voice therefore resounds with singular power and his views, speeches and criticisms are heard over the radio, seen on television screens and read in newspapers by millions.

Only a few years ago Solzhenitsyn was known in the West and in the Soviet Union only as an outstanding writer, a laureate of the

Nobel Prize for Literature. Of his political views and beliefs one could judge only indirectly by analysing and interpreting his literary writings. His political programme, as defined in his famous letter to the Fourth Congress of Soviet writers in 1967, confined itself to demanding the abolition of censorship for literary works, and it met with widespread support among Soviet writers and intelligentsia. In his works published in 1962-6 in the Soviet Union, as well as in those circulating in samizdat form, one could not find any anti-Communist ideas or anti-Soviet statements. Moreover, in his story "For the Good of the Cause" published in 1963, the chief positive hero was a Party activist, the secretary of a city committee of the Soviet Communist Party. In his novel *Cancer Ward* attentive readers have found a defence of "ethical socialism" and a picture of the Soviet Union gradually emerging from the horrors of Stalinism to enter a period of normal human life. In point of fact, in 1964 Solzhenitsyn was put forward as a candidate for the Lenin Prize for Literature and he actively collaborated with the editorial board of *Novy Mir,* which did its best to get him the prize. But to judge by what one learns from his autobiographical book, *The Calf Butted the Oak,* published in 1975, all this was nothing else but make-believe, a game, the purpose of which was to conceal his real thoughts and his real work, above all, his work on *Gulag Archipelago,* a three-volume historical investigation in a literary form of the entire field of oppression in the Soviet Union starting in 1918.

Having found himself unexpectedly in the West, Solzhenitsyn has been able to throw off his dissembling and publish works in which he openly proclaims his views, sympathies and antipathies. These works, being the creation of a great writer, will remain the object of interest for many years to come, while a number of them have already provoked an animated discussion among sections of the Soviet intelligentsia — a discussion in which I too have been able to take part by contributing several articles. However, since 1975 Solzhenitsyn has acted no longer as a writer but chiefly as a political agitator, making speeches, giving interviews and holding press conferences on a wide range of problems.

Being without access to a wide range of Western newspapers and journals, I cannot analyse and examine all the statements and ideas which Solzhenitsyn has expressed in his many speeches. Moreover, Solzhenitsyn has declared on many occasions that his views have been distorted by the press. However, Soviet dissidents have been able to acquaint themselves with his slim book entitled *American Speeches,* which Solzhenitsyn published in the Russian language in Paris in the autumn of 1975. In this book, which will no doubt be translated into many languages, we find the text of the three speeches which Solzhenitsyn delivered in the United States in the summer of 1975, namely, his speech in Washington on June 30, his speech in New York on July 9 and his speech to the US Senate on July 15, 1975. It is in connection with these speeches that I want to make a number of critical comments.

One cannot avoid polemicising with Solzhenitsyn for the simple reason that he has taken it upon himself, as a rule, to speak in his latest speeches in the name of the entire Russian people or in the name of his entire generation or, a little more modestly, in the name of all former prisoners in the USSR. As he puts it, " . . . in the name of all those who shared with me my forced labour . . . and in the name of those who are working today in our country in conditions of oppression . . . " (p.11).

There can be no doubt that in an important part of his literary creativity Solzhenitsyn has mirrored the terrible upheavals and tragedies of Russia's post-revolutionary history. Moreover, Solzhenitsyn's great artistic talent has exerted an influence on the growth of public consciousness in the Soviet Union after 1962. But this does not mean that the growth of public consciousness in our country has been along the same line as Solzhenitsyn's own ideological evolution. Solzhenitsyn is deeply mistaken when he claims that he is speaking in the name of the majority of the Russian people. Neither a majority of the workers, nor of the intelligentsia, nor of the former prisoners, and not even a majority of the yet weak opposition to the existing régime in the Soviet Union, shares his basic ideas, judgements, forecasts and prophecies. The one-sided and tendentious nature of his speeches is turning Solzhenitsyn increasingly into a solitary figure. He is not only not seeking allies among the well known personalities of the Russian emigration or the internal opposition in the Soviet Union, but he has in fact, broken off all personal and business relations with his former friends and the people who shared his ideas.

Solzhenitsyn's one-sidedness and narrow-mindedness are strikingly apparent in his chief guiding thought which like a red thread runs through all his recent speeches. His guiding thought is that every-thing evil – or *almost* everything evil – in our world is concentrated in the socialist states of Eastern Europe and therefore the West must unite against this evil and force it to retreat. [("I have come to tell you about my experiences over there . . . " where "the evil of the world, hostile to mankind, is concentrated" (p.87).]

One cannot deny that in our life in the Soviet Union there existed in the past and there continues to exist much that is evil, although the conception of what is good or evil is not one on which many people will yet agree. However, the East and, in particular, the Soviet Union, do not enjoy a monopoly of evil whatever one under-stands it to be. Regrettably, evil in all its forms is distributed rather equally all over the earth and the West, naturally enough, is not the paragon of justice and all virtues. Only forty years ago it was the prosperous West that kept under its domination the major part of Asia, Africa and Latin America and brute force was the main instru-ment used by the West to maintain its power. Nor was it by a voluntary act of justice that the West withdrew from the countries of the so-called Third World. Democratic France, even after having suffered a defeat in Indochina, carried on a long and a bloody war in Algeria, during which the country was covered with concentra-tion camps and torture became commonplace. Over a million Alger-ians out of a total population of nine millions died in that war. And is it not a fact that Western Europe was the breeding ground of the two World Wars, the first of which resulted in the triumph of the October Revolution, which Solzhenitsyn in vain attempts to depict as the cause of all the misfortunes suffered by the Russian people. As for the Second World War, it has brought the world not only tens of millions of dead, but also many new revolutions and revolutionary wars.

The Western world is even today torn by contradictions and injustices and their existence feeds all the left-wing movements in the West. The millions of Italian and French Communists did not emigrate to their countries from the Soviet Union.

In his attacks on the Communists and all left-wingers in the West Solzhenitsyn has been singularly prejudiced. He speaks, for instance, with undisguised venom of the Portuguese Communists and does not miss any opportunity to gibe at Mario Soares, the leader of the Portuguese Socialists, and the Revolutionary Military

Council of Portugal. But he cannot find a single word to condemn the 45 years of dictatorship by Salazar and Caetano, and the 15 years of colonial wars waged by the two dictators in Africa, the chief cause of the Portuguese revolution.

Dealing with the origins of the Soviet system, Solzhenitsyn writes that it came to power by means of an armed coup, that it created the Cheka, that it introduced executions by firing squad without a trial, that it suppressed peasant uprising, and so on. To the Soviet system he opposed "the wide and stable American way of life".

But was not the American Democracy born in revolution and violence? And was not the very birth of the United States preceded by a long and cruel war with Britain, which ended not only with the victory of the American Colonies, but also with the expulsion of hundreds of thousands of Loyalists, who were deprived of their rights as citizens and were forced to emigrate to Canada, the West Indies and Britain? And is it not a fact that, even after the creation of the United States, there were many little wars with the Indians, who were not only tortured, but also burned alive and killed in their thousands in order to clear the land for settlement by white Europeans and their Negro slaves? And did not the formal abolition of slavery (which, may we recall, came a few years after the abolition of serfdom in Russia) necessitate the waging of a civil war lasting four years, in which the South mobilised over a million men and the North over 2,500,000 men? And can one approve the methods used by the FBI and CIA for the suppression and demoralisation of oppositional groups in the United States over the last 20 years? Or does Solzhenitsyn believe that in the struggle against the Left all means are justified?

Solzhenitsyn has forecast that, after the departure of the American troops from Southern Vietnam, millions of South Vietnamese will be shot or put in concentration camps. (His forecasts have not been justified so far and, we may hope, will prove wrong.) But Solzhenitsyn has not even mentioned the millions of ordinary Vietnamese who were killed or wounded as a result of American bombings. However great the shortcomings of the Communist régime in Vietnam, it is the Communists who knew how to lead the national-liberation and anti-colonialist war of the Vietnamese people. This resulted in victory just as 200 years ago many similar ideas of national independence ensured that the American Colonies should win independence from Britain.

While condemning — and justifiably — the notorious Berlin Wall, Solzhenitsyn calls on the West to create a gigantic, impassable wall around the Soviet Union and other socialist states, and to stop trading, as well as all economic, technical and cultural exchanges and cooperation with them. But this is the kind of advice that if accepted by the West would prove fatal to its own social order. It is true indeed that Soviet society is in many ways a sick society. But its illnesses are far from fatal. *And therefore even a total isolation of the Soviet Union from the West will not lead to the fall of the Soviet régime that Solzhenitsyn hates so much, but will only strengthen the most reactionary circles, the most reactionary views and institutions in the Soviet Union.* The West too may suffer badly from a resurgence of such a savage confrontation and isolation. For this would happen at a time when Western society itself is not particularly healthy and strong, contrary to what Solzhenitsyn believes. Is it not likely that such a total confrontation between the West and the East might lead to a violent and dangerous crisis of all the "Western" illnesses, weaknesses and diseases?

Oddly enough, not so long ago Solzhenitsyn in his "Letter to the Soviet Leaders" implored them to do everything in their power to avoid an *ideological* war with China. Yet today Solzhenitsyn is appealing to the West to start a savage ideological war with the Soviet Union, which from a cold war could easily turn into a real hot war. What would then happen to the tens of millions of young Russians, the mainstay of the Russian nation, about whose fate Solzhenitsyn worried so much when he painted his apocalyptic picture of what would occur if it came to war with China? Or are we to understand that in order to destroy the communist ideology even the sacrifice of their lives would not be too much?

When speaking to American audiences, Solzhenitsyn expounded to them not only his views, but he also gave them his advice and forecasts. Often he tried to back up his forecasts by quoting historical facts. Unfortunately, his "facts" are all too often crude falsifications of history and, in most cases, they are premeditated ones. This, by the way, is the typical method used by Soviet propaganda of the old style; which worked on the principle that one may say what one likes of one's opponent.

On two occasions Solzhenitsyn told American audiences that "during the years preceding the Revolution, the entire Communist Party in Russia was led by Shlyapnikov and not by Lenin, who was abroad." And again: "And I remind you: before the Revolution the Communist Party in Russia was led by Shlyapnikov, not by Lenin". This, of course, is complete rubbish: Shlyapnikov did not play any important part in the leadership and the shaping of the policies of the Bolsheviks, whereas the leader of the party − and the leader was nobody else but Lenin − did not cease to lead it irrespective of whether he was in his own country or abroad.

Solzhenitsyn told the American audiences of a pamphlet published in 1918, which contains the minutes of the meetings of the workers of a *number* of Petrograd factories. Solzhenitsyn asserts, however, that "this is a detailed record of a meeting of all the representatives of the Petrograd factories and works . . . I repeat, all the representatives of the Petrograd factories and works cursed the Communists, who had let them down in all their promises". (p.12). But the pamphlet in question clearly states that it is the record of a meeting *not of all* the representatives of the Petrograd workers, but of those who supported the Mensheviks and Social Revolutionaries. The meeting was held in the Menshevik Club under the chairmanship of Ye. S. Berg, a right-wing Social Revolutionary, and among the speakers there were several members of the Central Committee of the Menshevik Party. The meeting did not in any way reflect the state of mind of the mass of Petrograd workers. Although in the spring of 1918 the workers of Petrograd had many good reasons to be dissatisfied, in particular with the economic situation, it is a historical fact that the overwhelming majority of the workers in Petrograd and other industrial centres in Russia supported the Bolsheviks and Lenin. It was of those workers that the *volunteer* units of the Red Guards and later the Red Army were formed in the first months after the Revolution. It was their support that helped the Bolsheviks to stay in power during the most difficult months of 1918, when the majority of the peasants, Cossacks and petty town landlords rose against them. The power of the Bolsheviks in the years 1918-1920 was indubitably exerted by a minority and Lenin did not conceal this fact. Nevertheless, the working class provided the Bolsheviks with a sufficiently reliable social basis for their exercise of power.

There is no need to disprove Solzhenitsyn's claim that the biggest constructions of the First Five Year Plan were created *exclusively* with the help of American technology and American materials and that Stalin himself had admitted, according to Solzhenitsyn, that two-thirds of everything had come from the West. It is true, of course, that Western technology and Western credits played a very important part in the First Five Year Plan. But there was nothing philanthropic about the West's supply of either. On the contrary, there was a form of economic collaboration from which the West derived many advantages. For those were the years when the West suffered from the greatest economic and financial crisis in its history.

When speaking of the cruelties of the Civil War in Russia, Solzhenitsyn recalled to the American audiences only the horrors of the Red Terror. But it would be possible to compile an even longer list of atrocities committed by the Whites and the armies of the interventionists, including the British, the French, the Americans and the Japanese, who sent their armies to Russia not in order to feed the hungry workers and peasants.

Solzhenitsyn's speeches abound in many contradictions and absurdities. The capitalists, by the way, do not fare any better in his speeches than the Communists. Thus in his speech of June 30, 1975, to a huge gathering in the Washington Hilton, Solzhenitsyn attacked "the craving for easy gain that is burning up the capitalists and is beyond all reason, all limits of self-control, all conscience and knows only how to make more money". But this is precisely what Karl Marx used to say. Solzhenitsyn, however, reminds us of the self-seeking of capitalists not in order to explain that this craving for easy profits was responsible for the seizure of colonies or the countless wars in the 19th and 20th centuries. On the contrary. By this craving for easy profits Solzhenitsyn has attempted to explain the policy of trading, cooperation and détente with the Soviet Union, which is also supported by a large section of the business world in the West. In his indignation at détente Solzhenitsyn even recalls the Marxist slogan of "Proletarians of all countries — unite!" and appeals to all Americans as "brothers in labour" to act both against the Soviet Communists and their own capitalists, who allegedly have allied themselves with the Communist leaders.

Similarly Solzhenitsyn condemned in his speeches the alliance between the Western Democracies and the Soviet Union in 1941 and explained it as due to the fact that the West wanted to set the two totalitarian régimes of Nazi Germany and Stalin's Russia at each other's throats. However, according to Solzhenitsyn, as a result of the self-seeking that is inherent in capitalism the Western Democracies were unable to foresee the results of their actions and therefore came a cropper. Such an explanation of the policies of the West is not very original or novel — one finds it in Stalin's explanation of his policies at the time. But what really matters is not what Solzhenitsyn actually told his American audiences, but what he did not say aloud. Namely, in his opinion it would have been better if the Western Democracies had helped Germany to smash the Soviet Union.

"The United States", Solzhenitsyn told his American audiences, "has proved itself for a long time to be the most magnanimous and generous country in the world . . . During the last war help for Soviet people — warm clothes, food, gifts — was collected in all the states . . . But we never saw it, let alone received any of it. The gifts were distributed in the privileged circles and nobody told us about it". (p.39). This is an outright lie. I do not dispute that part of the American gifts ended up among "the privileged circles", but most of it went to the works, factories and establishments engaged in war production. In the works in Tbilisi, where I spent the best time of the war, there were many workers and employees who received American gifts. Later in Moscow and Leningrad I met people who certainly did not belong to the "privileged circles" and were still wearing American clothes received many years before.

Solzhenitsyn condemns the self-seeking and craving for easy profits of the capitalists, but forgets to mention that the capitalists are not the least important people in the West and that consequently it is this very same craving that has been responsible for the injustices and defects of capitalist society, which gave birth to the socialist and communist movements of the 19th and 20th centuries. No, Solzhenitsyn keeps all his condemnation for socialism and communism.

It would be difficult to dispute many of Solzhenitsyn's criticisms of the existing socialist states. It is absolutely true that in our country we have no real elections, no independent press and no truly free political, scientific or literary activities. It is absolutely true that in our country we have no independent judiciary or trade unions free of Party control. However, Solzhenitsyn has not made the slightest effort to analyse the difference between the concrete attempts up to date to create socialist societies and the ideals of socialism, which are the product of the eternal human striving to build a just social system in which all people can achieve their own kind of happiness. Solzhenitsyn refuses to admit that the reason why communism triumphed in the 20th century first in such countries as Russia and China was because in these countries the sufferings of tens and even hundreds of millions of people were particularly great, and therefore the striving of the oppressed millions to create a better social system was particularly powerful. But for Solzhenitsyn there is no difference at all between the ideals of socialism and their actual implementation. No, to him socialism and communism are evil incarnate in all its forms and manifestations.

"Communism", Solzhenitsyn said in one of his speeches, "is a gross attempt to explain human society and man". (p.63). Yes, it is quite true that contemporary communism contains within itself much that is still gross and tentative. So far even many of Marx's and Engels's ideas have not found their realisation in the existing communist states. Moreover, Marxism itself is not by any means the final achievement of the human mind. It represents only the starting point in man's attempts to explain scientifically the history of human society and it inescapably contains much that is utopian, fortuitous and unscientific. But what other theory presents us with a subtler and more precise explanation of contemporary society? Does Christianity offer a better explanation? But Christianity is even less precise and less scientific; it is accepted by only a minority of mankind and in our own time it has fewer followers than Marxism. Moreover, the contemporary social, political and ethical life of the west has departed even further from the teachings of Jesus Christ than contemporary Soviet society has departed from the teachings of Marx, Engels, Lenin and the programme of the Soviet Communist Party.

"Marxism", Solzhenitsyn tells us, "has always been opposed to freedom". (p.63). And he attempts to prove his argument by having recourse to the method of historical falsification worked out by I. Shafarevich in his collection of papers entitled *From Under the Rubble.* Solzhenitsyn quotes out of context several sentences from the writings of the young Engels, which were written a year before he met Marx, i.e., several years before Marx himself became a Marxist, as it were. Moreover, Engels's critique of bourgeois political freedoms — a critique that is indeed too sharp because Engels allowed himself to be carried away into one-sidedness — Solzhenitsyn tries to present as a critique of *all* political freedoms, and Engels's critique of the bourgeois democracy in contemporary Britain — a critique also not entirely justified and tendentious — as a critique of *every* form of democracy. Yet how indignant Solzhenitsyn was when in 1967 the Union of Soviet Writers wanted to publish his old, "long abandoned" play "The Victors' Feast" in order to confront his views in the play with his latest opinions. "This play", Solzhenitsyn stated at a meeting of the Secretariat of the Union of Soviet Writers, "has nothing to do with my present writings. I am as little responsible for this play today as many men of letters would now wish to repeat their speeches and write again the books they had made or written in 1949". Yet today Solzhenitsyn does not shrink from using the same unfair trick to discredit Marx and Engels. The fact is that in his war against Marxism Solzhenitsyn believes that the end justifies any means.

We remember how in the first volume of *Gulag Archipelago* Alexandr Solzhenitsyn gibed at Lenin's formula that "morality is what serves to destroy the old exploiting society and to unite all workers around the proletariat, which will create a new society of communists". There is no arguing that Lenin's formula was far from successful and that it cannot serve as a foundation for a truly communist morality. Such a moral relativism, in accordance with which everything is moral that is beneficial to "the cause of the proletariat" — and who can define what is beneficial? — cannot but harm the cause of socialism and communism in the final analysis.

But how does Solzhenitsyn's understanding of what is moral differ from Lenin's definition? He told his American audiences: "what is opposed to Communism — that's what common humanity is!" (p.65) But this is Lenin's formula, except that it is even worse and turned inside out. "Common humanity" may be identified with the Tiger Cages in South Vietnam, with the carpet bombings of civilian populations, with the White Terror in the years of our own Civil War, with the underground dungeons used by the Portuguese Secret Police, with the Nazi concentration camps. After all, they have all been used "in the struggle against communism."

"Communism is indivisible", Solzhenitsyn tells the world. "The sun of the Comintern has not set. Its energy has been converted into electricity and electricity has gone into underground cables . . . The visible differences between Communist Parties are only apparent . . ." (p.70). He makes fun of the words of Olof Palme, the leader of the Swedish Social Democrats, that "Communism can survive only by adopting democratic positions". (p.71). Communism, Solzhenitsyn believes, is completely incompatible with democracy. One must not conclude any kind of agreements with communism. The only answer to the challenge of the communist world must be the unification of the West and the building up of its military potential. Communism can be broken only by the use of force and Solzhenitsyn calls on the West to do it as soon as possible, while the United States and other Western countries still possess economic and military superiority. To speak of the morality of such views or the Christianity of such a prophet would be a waste of time. But we may point out that to the most devoted but wise apologists of capitalism it must be clear that Alexandr Solzhenitsyn is late with his appeals by several decades.

Solzhenitsyn has spent only two years in the West. In these two years he has come to the conclusion that Western civilisation is on the decline and giving up one position after another. But which are the countries he quotes as examples of how Western Democracy is losing one position after another? The countries he spoke of in his recent interview on British television as having "lost their freedom" and fallen into the hands of "tyrants", "puppets" and "bandits" are Vietnam, Laos, China, Angola. Since when have these countries been part of "Western Civilisation"? Perhaps since the time when colonial régimes were established in them by means far from pacific? When did these countries enjoy "democracy and freedom"? They never enjoyed either. It may be said that none of these countries know democracy and freedom today, but at least they are free of colonial oppression, the greatest evil of our times.

Western civilisation, which Solzhenitsyn called in his London interview "the sun of freedom", has grown over centuries in the shape of colonial powers, warring in the first place among themselves. The Russian Revolution was the result of these conflicts. Nor was the Second World War started by the Soviet Union. Already in 1940 there practically remained nothing of the Western Democracies in Europe — only Britain was saved by the Channel from the New Order on the Continent and the Channel was only a temporary defence. One may hate the Soviet system and the principles of socialism, but one cannot but recognise the historical truth that without Russia's participation in the Second World War there would be no "Free World" in Western Europe. Solzhenitsyn forgets that not only the Russians have a tragic experience of totalitarianism — a dictatorship no less cruel than our own was experienced within the memory of our generation by practically all the countries in Western Europe.

This tragic period in our history is finished. So has gradually come to an end the Cold War period lasting almost two decades, which the West waged "from positions of strength". The West lost the Cold War at the same time as it lost its "positions of strength" — and this cannot be reversed. Today there is no other alternative but the road of peaceful cooperation. The reason why socialism in Russia right from its beginning adopted savage and totalitarian forms was to a large extent due to the fact that it was born and developed in a hostile encirclement. That kind of hostility is practically non-existent in the West today and this fact does not strengthen but, on the contrary, weakens the arguments of the partisans of a "tough line" towards the Soviet Union. Should we therefore rekindle the old hostility in the hope that a return to the Cold War may help the Russian people to build a more democratic society? Certainly not. Such a course could only result in disaster for everybody.

April 1976